Congress Shall Make No Law

Congress

Shall Make No Law

Oliver Wendell Holmes,
the First Amendment,
and Judicial
Decision Making

JEREMY COHEN

Iowa State University Press / Ames

JEREMY COHEN is Assistant Professor of Communication
at Stanford University, Stanford, California.

© 1989 Iowa State University Press, Ames, Iowa 50010

FRONTISPIECE: Justice Oliver Wendell Holmes (Courtesy of the Library of Congress).

Composed by Iowa State University Press
Printed in the United States of America

First edition, 1989

Library of Congress Cataloging-in-Publication Data

Cohen, Jeremy, 1949–
    Congress shall make no law: Oliver Wendell Holmes, the First Amendment, and judicial decision making / Jeremy Cohen. — 1st ed.
        p. cm.
    Bibliography: p.
    Includes index.
    ISBN 0-8138-0022-6
    1. Freedom of speech — United States. 2. Freedom of the press — United States. 3. Holmes, Oliver Wendell, 1841–1935. 4. United States. Supreme Court. 5. Judicial process — United States.
    I. Title.
    KF4770.C64 1989
    342.73′0853 — dc19
    [347.306853]   88–12793
                                                                                          CIP

For my wife, Catherine
and our children,
Leah and Joshua.

Contents

Foreword

AS the United States prepares for the bicentennial of the Bill of Rights, which will be celebrated in 1991, the need for a more comprehensive and better-focused understanding of free expression becomes increasingly urgent. As changes occur in the membership of the Supreme Court of the United States, as well as elsewhere in the federal judiciary, those who care about freedom of expression and, especially, freedom of the press worry that the lack of a unified theory will lead not only to bad case law, but to an intolerable intrusion on a fundamental freedom that constitutes the nation's communication system.

These commentators and others who disagree sharply with them see conflicting rights wherein the institutional media confront individuals. The freedom to disseminate information sometimes collides with the right to privacy and other personal liberties.

Though this has long been a problem for citizens and constitutional lawyers alike, its importance is deepened by the rise of an information society. In a period when the maxim that Information Is Power and as such traditional institutions as the family, the church, and the school seemingly have less vitality and strength, not to mention influence, the media and their rights become more central to human discourse.

Some defenders of First Amendment press rights steer a narrow course, looking in reductionist fashion at a short line of cases stretching only back to World War I and on which much of present-day jurisprudence is based. They see communication law as a preeminent part of constitutional law and often they have little interest in or sympathy for the larger contours of the law that touch on such fields as criminal law, property law, or civil procedure. To those with such a view, nearly any impediment to the rights of the press is unacceptable and ought to be overcome. On the other side are scholars, commentators, and citizen-critics who give the First Amendment short shrift. To them it is not the first and preeminent freedom, but rather one of many rights that must live in harmony with competing interests.

To this debate Jeremy Cohen brings new insights and a fresh

perspective on one of the linchpins of our understanding of freedom of expression. At first glance, it would appear that he is looking at the role of one justice, the storied Oliver Wendell Holmes, Jr., and one case, the seminal *Schenck v. United States* but the study presented here is much more. While Professor Cohen rigorously pursues the meaning of a great constitutional law case wherein the modern Supreme Court began to sketch out First Amendment law, he uses a singular instance to expand and extend our theory of freedom of expression. He does so by challenging existing assumptions about the role of Justice Holmes, who wrote the majority opinion in the landmark case. By understanding Justice Holmes's legal philosophy, values, and beliefs, Professor Cohen argues that we can illuminate our view of the evolution of the First Amendment.

Because there was no earlier High Court interpretation of the First Amendment, the Schenck case, which involved the advocacy of illegal action by two Socialists, stands as the first in the line of cases that taken together constitute our law of press and speech. Before constitutional scholars have always looked to the "bottom line" intent of the Supreme Court in the case with little attention either to the context of the times or to the process of the decision.

It is here that Jeremy Cohen breaks new ground, arguing that the process or the *how* of this great decision may be just as important as the *what* of the decision. Thus, he looks at the Supreme Court's jurisprudence and the special role of Justice Holmes as an intellectual leader. This approach allows room for a new interpretation of the meaning of freedom of expression. Professor Cohen takes his readers on a journey into the intricacies of the thinking of the Supreme Court then and now as well as the context of the case as it confronted and abutted other areas of the law. The book is a highly readable adventure in legal interpretation involving violations of espionage law and a search for constitutional principles. Along the way we see Justice Holmes and his black-robed brethren and gain insight into his intellectual development and constitutional faith. We confront the question that Professor Cohen believes crucial: Did Holmes base his opinion in *Schenck* on the First Amednement? This is not simply the stuff of legal footnotes, but a linchpin in our concept of the First Amendment. Jeremy Cohen effectively demolishes previous interpretations as he concludes that *Schenck* was not essentially a First Amendment case.

Such an analysis does not pull the plug on the First Amendment, but instead broadens its evolution and development in modern court decisions. It argues for the idea that the First Amendment must always be seen in league with other legal theories—with property law, criminal law, and civil procedure. Cohen's view of the First Amendment is therefore far more textured than the traditional linear theories that derive from a narrow reading of *Schenck*. And, ultimately, it is a First Amendment more user friendly than one that opts for freedom of expression above all other rights. There is more latitude for citizens to advance their claims to free speech and free press in the context of competing interests. It does not close debate, but widens its scope. Finally, Cohen's thesis gives rise to the often-overlooked importance of state courts and the way that they forge a theory of freedom of expression at a level in which it affects individuals and institutions.

Jeremy Cohen's examination is more than new wine in old bottles, but a skillful use of the tools of the media scholar, the historian, and the legal scholar in an integrated fashion. Few legal scholars have thought in these terms and here Professor Cohen's training as a communication researcher, also schooled in legal history, is especially valuable. He avoids the pitfalls of those who become myopic cheerleaders for the First Amendment, by pursuing a somewhat heretical route to a conclusion. Along the way he rejects a simplistic and ultimately dangerous interpretation. It is my hope that this provocative book will stimulate much debate about the First Amendment and also generate additional studies.

EVERETTE E. DENNIS
Executive Director
Gannett Center for Media Studies
Columbia University, New York City

Acknowledgments

MANY people and events have influenced my work on this book. The legal issues were first raised in conversation with Professor Don Pember at the University of Washington. He suggested a dissertation and a book and taught me the value of context in legal research. Professor Richard Carter explained that there is nothing difficult about writing a dissertation. It's just that by the time you learn how, he said, you never have to do it again. The lessons of how, and how not to write a dissertation, generated this book. Professors Wallace Loh and Roger Simpson read numerous early drafts and provided useful commentary. Appreciation is also due to communication historians Gerald Baldasty and William Ames. Their teaching enabled me to identify and find the material I needed.

I also wish to thank Dean Edward Bassett at the Medill School of Journalism for his continued encouragement and guidance, and Everette E. Dennis, Executive Director at the Gannett Center for Media Studies, for his careful reading of the manuscript and his welcome suggestions for changes and additions.

Professor Timothy Gleason at the University of Oregon deserves special thanks for the numerous hours he willingly spent with me discussing case analysis and constitutional theory. His careful study of nineteenth-century American jurisprudence provided valuable insight.

The students in my seminars and lecture courses at the University of Oregon and at Stanford University also have provided significant assistance. Special recognition goes to Greg Kerber, Faith Perry, and Lisa Trimingham for their assistance with the research and their tireless efforts to track missing cites and elusive newspaper reports of the Schenck trial.

The University of Washington provided a generous dissertation fellowship. Trudy Flynn, always on my side, helped me through the hoops to get research funding and was a constant source of friendship. The William Randolph Hearst Foundation provided a generous financial gift that allowed me the time and resources to continue my research while at Stanford University. Both have earned my gratitude.

Buffalo Springfield sang a song in 1966, "For What It's Worth."
Stephen Stills wrote,

> What a field day for the heat.
> A thousand people in the street.
> Singing songs and a carrying signs.
> Mostly saying hurray for our side.
>
> Think it's time we stopped, children
> What's that sound?
> Everybody look what's going down.

Their song, together with the unintentional help of my high school principal, the Los Angeles Police assigned to the Vietnam War demonstration at Century City Plaza on June 23, 1967, and president S. I. Hayakawa at San Francisco State College, provided my first awareness that freedom of expression—even protected by the constitutional recognition of the relation of unabridged speech to democratic governance—is a very fragile gift.

Dr. Joseph Barankin was also at San Francisco State and is now with the California Department of Education. I trust he will accept this as the paper I still owe him and accept my gratitude for his sensitivity to diverse opinion.

I also acknowledge *American Journalism* for publishing my article, *"Schenck v. United States:* A Reexamination," which was an earlier version of some of the material contained in this book. Editor David Sloan at the University of Alabama, Little Rock, deserves special thanks.

Love and appreciation is also extended, of course, to my wife and children, Catherine Jordan and Leah and Joshua Cohen, and to my parents, Ruth and Ernest Cohen.

I appreciate the help of Iowa State University Press. Managing editor Bill Silag patiently answered my queries and followed through on my needs. Gavin Lockwood did an exemplary job of copy editing.

Finally, if any of the thinking is clouded, the facts subject to more careful or more useful interpretation, or the citations amiss, the fault is mine and mine alone.

JEREMY COHEN
Department of Communication
Stanford University

Congress Shall Make No Law

1

Introduction

Why for instance, should it be said that the liberty of the press shall not be restrained, when no power is given by which restrictions may be imposed? I will not contend that such a provision would confer a regulating power; but it is evident that it would furnish to men disposed to usurp, a plausible pretense for claiming that power.

ALEXANDER HAMILTON, 1788,
No. 84, *The Federalist Papers*

THE constitutional guarantees of speech, press, and political dissent are contained in the First Amendment, to be sure. They are no less the product, however, of judicial interpretations of the Bill of Rights developed by Supreme Court justices of varying legal philosophies and beliefs. Their interpretations of just what the First Amendment means, or was intended to mean, have only a short history. The value of a free press was well understood in North America long before the constitutional press clause was drafted. More than two thousand newspapers were established between 1690 and 1820.[1] The United States Supreme Court, however, was not presented with a case involving the freedoms of speech, press, and political dissent until 1919—thirteen decades after its founding—when Elizabeth Baer and Charles Schenck appealed their conviction of violating the antisedition laws.[2] Their case is known as *Schenck v. United States.*

In a sense, Justice Oliver Wendell Holmes, Jr., and the other eight members of the Court who decided the 1919 *Schenck* case, seemed to have a clean slate on which to sketch their interpretations of the First Amendment. No earlier Supreme Court considerations of sedition needed to be defended or explained, no prior High Court interpretation of the First Amendment tied the justices to a single, narrow approach. There was, in short, no important First Amendment precedent.

Just how free then were Holmes and his colleagues to shape the meaning of the constitutional prohibition of laws abridging freedom of speech? What brought the Court to conclude that the First Amendment did not shield Schenck's seditious speech from congressional sanction and punishment? The equation is complex. It contains the forty-five words that make up the single sentence that is the First Amendment. It also contains the jurisprudence of the men who reached that decision, jurisprudence that in fact prevented the justices from breathing life into a tolerant constitutional doctrine of freedom of expression.

Legal scholars, historians, and others interested in individual liberties have long studied the First Amendment implications of *Schenck v. United States*. What constitutional precedent is established for future battles between freedom of expression and governmental interest in reduced public debate? What does *Schenck* add to our historical knowledge and appreciation of our approach as a nation to freedom of expression?

Little or no attention has been given, however, to the judicial process from which the *Schenck* decision was molded. We have been ready to accept *Schenck* as a First Amendment case without stopping to consider the possibility that it only *looked* like a First Amendment case. Indeed, the case had all the earmarks. It concerned the prohibition of speech, prohibition that we would recognize today as an abridgment of constitutionally guaranteed rights. The defense attorneys presented briefs to the Court that championed, explicitly, the First Amendment rights of their clients and challenged the Court to uphold those rights. The Court talked about the First Amendment in its opinion. Yet the judicial decision-making process that produced *Schenck* lends little support to a constitutional analysis of the case.

It is the judicial process by which the Court came to sanction congressional abridgment of speech that is the focus of this book. And it is the examination of that process that ultimately suggests that we have been too quick to see *Schenck* as an example of First Amendment analysis by the judiciary—even though *Schenck* undoubtedly helped to shape judicial attitudes about the meaning of the First Amendment for years to come.

The need to recognize the importance of the judicial process as a shaping force upon our theories of freedom of expression and the First Amendment motivates this book. The judicial process requires us to explore and to understand the role of Supreme Court justices and the limits placed upon those women and men by the realities, political and constitutional, of a tripartite system of government. The temptation is always present to assume that because the First Amendment forbids congressional actions that trample speech, press, and peaceful political dissent, the courts will have little difficulty spreading the constitutional umbrella that protects expression from state sanctioned interference. Experience teaches, however, that even First Amendment absolutists such as Justices William O. Douglas and Hugo Black found exceptions to the command, Congress shall make no law. In the end, the procedures of constitutional jurisprudence and the political and constitutional limits upon judicial decision making may have as much to do with the legal parameters of freedom of expression as do the actual words of the First Amendment. Only by understanding the role of the Court, the role of the Court's justices, and the limits that weigh upon their actions can we begin to fully comprehend the meaning of their decisions.

Competing Theories of Decision Making

It has been said many times that we cannot be sure exactly what the constitutional drafters intended the First Amendment to mean.[3] At the two hundredth anniversary of the Bill of Rights the debate is no less boisterous and no less important than it was at the Constitution's Philadelphia inception. Constitutional experts, such as Supreme Court Justice Thurgood Marshall, go so far as to question the wisdom of relying at all on the original intent of the constitutional framers, who did not recognize the rights of women and who continenced the institution of racial slavery. In a speech recognizing the two hundredth anniversary of the Constitution, Marshall said, "I do not believe that the meaning of the Constitution was forever 'fixed' at the Philadelphia convention. Nor do I find the wisdom, foresight and sense of justice exhibited by the framers particularly profound. To the contrary, the government they devised was defective from the start, requiring several amendments, a civil war and momentous social transformation to attain the system of constitutional government, and its respect for the individual freedoms and human rights, we hold as fundamental today."[4]

Others are not so ready to set the past aside. Chief Justice William Rehnquist, for example, suggests that the Constitution, although it could not foresee the future, in fact provides the basis of answers to current legal questions. He counsels seeking out the *original intent* of the constitutional drafters. "Merely because a particular activity may not have existed when the Constitution was adopted," Rehnquist said, "or because the framers could not have conceived of a particular method of transacting affairs, cannot mean that the general language of the Constitution may not be applied to such a course of conduct."[5]

Justices Marshall and Rehnquist illustrate two dimensions of the arena in which constitutional issues, such as freedom of expression, are today considered. Opposing, sometimes contradictory convictions about the role of the judiciary and the degrees of freedom available to those charged with interpreting the basic document of government create an atmosphere of intellectual tension. The approaches of the two men are unlikely to develop agreement on issues. Their views of the judicial branch of government speak directly to the decisions they make about what the government may and may not do. Justice Marshall and Chief Justice Rehnquist clearly illustrate the fact that it is insufficient to examine only the operationalization of law. Those interested in our civil rights must also understand the subtleties of the process by which the law is operationalized. Just as we need to explore the meaning and application of the First Amendment, we need to understand the meaning and application of the judicial role that underlies the foundation of First Amendment decisions. We need to understand how and why judges feel constrained within clearly identifiable boundaries that lead to decisions that may appear, substantively, as counterintuitive.

What we take the First Amendment to mean at the close of the twentieth century has roots, to no small extent, in the idea that under special circumstances — a clear and present danger, if you will — unabridged speech is too dangerous to tolerate. Given the importance of that idea, and its seeming defiance of the First Amendment, it is appropriate and necessary to consider the origins of judicially sanctioned exceptions to the constitutional command that "Congress shall make no law. . . ." *Schenck v. United States* marked the beginning of such exceptions on the Supreme Court and brought an unfortunate sense of prophecy and irony to Alexander Hamilton's 1788 fear that a guarantee of freedom, such as the First Amendment, committed to paper, might some day "furnish to men disposed to usurp, a plausible pretense for claiming that power."[6]

Alternative Explanations

The treatment of the First Amendment by the judiciary continues to have a great deal to do with the meaning of democracy. Our ability to question the official conduct of the government is a crucial element of the system of checks and balances designed to ensure the survival of self-government. With the given that *how* a judicial decision is made is just as important to our understanding of freedom as the *what* of that decision, the primary focus of this study is on *Schenck v. United States*. This was the United States Supreme Court's first experience with a challenge to a law that made it a crime against the government to publicly criticize national foreign policy. It was the Court's first opportunity to consider just what the framers meant by the words, "Congress shall make no law . . . abridging the freedom of speech, or of the press; or the right of the people peaceably to assemble, and to petition the Government for a redress of grievances."

Emphasis has often been placed on the actual suppression of speech and on the implications for speech present in the Supreme Court's *Schenck* decision, which spawned the famous "clear and present danger doctrine." Here the emphasis is on the Supreme Court's jurisprudence — that is, on the legal philosophy and procedural methodology used to decide the case. The Court's opinion was written by Justice Oliver Wendell Holmes, Jr. By examining his approach to the law and his view of the judicial role, it is possible to reach a new understanding of what *Schenck* means for freedom of expression.

Two questions must be raised about the specifics of Holmes's *Schenck* decision and a third question of a more general nature. First, is there any reason to suspect that Holmes did not base his judicial opinion on a careful consideration of the First Amendment? Next, can an alternative to the First Amendment explanation of *Schenck* be identified? And finally, what is the relation of the specific intricacies of the American judicial system—the judicial process—to any consideration of laws that may have an impact upon a citizen's freedom of speech? These questions will be answered in the following chapters, emphasizing the importance of the specific intricacies the American judicial system has to any consideration of the laws that impact upon a citizen's right to the freedoms of speech, press, and political dissent. The First Amendment is a bulwark in our democratic system of government, but it is not the only legal element involved when a citizen's right to speak clashes with conflicting values forwarded by government, business, and other special interest groups.

2

Scorn, Contumely, and Disrepute

Fear of serious injury cannot alone justify suppression of free
speech and assembly. Men feared witches and burnt women.

LOUIS BRANDEIS, 1927,
Whitney v. California

T HE United States Supreme Court upheld
a number of lower court decisions in 1919
to jail individuals under provisions of fed-
eral espionage and sedition legislation.[1] The 1917 Espionage Act
made it a crime to "willfully cause or attempt to cause insubordination, disloyalty, mutiny, or refusal of duty, in the military or naval
forces of the United States," or to "willfully obstruct the recruiting or
enlistment service."[2] Congress amended and strengthened the act the
following year. It became a federal crime to use language "intended to
bring the form of government of the United States into contempt,
scorn, contumely and disrepute," or to talk about the government in
terms that were "disloyal, scurrilous and abusive."[3]

Does the First Amendment ban on congressional legislation that
abridges speech vanish when the speaker is too scurrilous or abusive?

The most famous of the World War I sedition cases was *Schenck
v. United States,* based not so much on the notoriety or infamy of the
defendants as upon the Court's opinion written by Justice Oliver
Wendell Holmes, Jr. *Schenck* provided the High Court with its first
opportunity to consider the First Amendment. It was here that
Holmes created the well-known doctrine of "clear and present danger"

9

and here that the jurist coined the metaphor of comparing seditious speech to "falsely shouting fire in a theater and causing a panic." It is here, then, that it is appropriate to examine just how First Amendment guarantees of freedom of expression can envelop new ideas in a protective womb, or be set aside by courts and lawmakers who fear the impact of heretical speech.

The defendants in the case were Elizabeth Baer and Charles Schenck. They were Socialists whose crimes were, in essence, distributing circulars in 1917 that were critical of the draft and opposing the war in Europe. Their case was the first of its kind to reach the High Court and the first time in the Court's 130-year history that anyone attempted to hold the First Amendment up as a shield to government prosecution.

For Baer and Schenck, the First Amendment could not hold back the forces marshalled against them. The Supreme Court, in its premiere engagement with what would become a continuing confrontation between claims of national security and freedom of expression, stood united. The Court's nine justices voted unanimously to uphold the lower court convictions of the Socialists, which were punishable by fines of up to ten thousand dollars and terms in federal prison of up to twenty years.

Precursors

The crime of sedition or seditious libel dates at least as far back as thirteenth-century England, although speaking out against authority probably brought on dire consequences for the speaker long before organized governments began classifying the crime as such. In essence, sedition refers to a range of acts from criticism of the government or its representatives to calling for the organized overthrow of those in power. Punishment has ranged over the centuries from simple prison sentences, to torture, or hanging. Parliament made it a crime in 1275 to issue any "false news or tales whereby discord or occasion of discord or slander may grow between the king and his people or the great men of the realm."[4] In 1663 William Twyn discovered the full force triggered by the British Crown's fear of sedition and its impact upon the king's subjects. After publishing a book containing seditious libel and an endorsement of a right of revolution, Twyn was hanged, cut down, emasculated, disemboweled, quartered and, finally, beheaded.[5] Truth proved of little value as a defense until 1792 when Fox's Libel Act finally removed from British law the doctrine, "The greater the truth, the greater the libel."

Tolerance in America for divergent views—despite twentieth-century romantic notions of colonists and settlers bent on religious and political freedom for one and all—was limited. First Amendment historian Leonard Levy paints an unflattering portrait showing that the "persistent image of colonial America as a society in which freedom of expression was cherished is an hallucination of sentiment that ignores history."[6] Americans, Professor Levy wrote, "simply did not understand that freedom of thought and expression means equal freedom for the other fellow, especially the one with hated ideas."[7] Political scientist John Roche is also skeptical of frontier America as a tolerant society. Rather, Roche posits that "the individual liberty that was characteristic of early American society was a function of the openness and pluralism that was characteristic of the times rather than of any centralized libertarian ideology."[8] Communities tended to be homogeneous. Individuals holding differing political or religious beliefs were invited, politely or otherwise, to leave. Until the close of the nineteenth century, there seemed to be enough land to accommodate a plethora of individuals with divergent views.

While individuals and communities may have condoned conformity above conscience, the framers were unwilling to accept the risks of coerced cohesion. Written in 1787 and ratified December 15, 1791, the Bill of Rights of the United States Constitution contains the First Amendment, which speaks out directly against government suppression of speech. In addition to clauses separating church from state and providing for religious freedom, the First Amendment provides that "Congress shall make no law . . . abridging the freedom of speech, or of the press; or the right of the people peaceably to assemble, and to petition the Government for a redress of grievances." Less than a decade had passed when Congress set those words aside and declared seditious expression a crime against the government. Following close on the heels of the Alien Act, the Sedition Act became law on July 14, 1798. It became a criminal offense, not against the Crown, but the United States, to utter or publish false, scandalous, and malicious writings against the federal government with the intent of bringing the government into contempt or disrepute, or to stir up sedition against the government.

The American experience with sedition has long raised serious questions about what the framers of the Constitution intended the First Amendment to mean. There continues to be a plethora of opposing theories.[9] Most do assume that, at the least, the constitutional amendment was intended to cage any threat of prior restraint, while leaving open the possibility of punishment for speech beyond the continence of society. The only truly widespread agreement is that we may never know exactly what James Madison and his colleagues had in mind. Whatever the framers' intended meaning, the targets of congressional antisedition legislation were the critics of President John Adams during the anti-French hysteria of 1798. Jeffersonian newspaper editors opposed to a possible war with France, Congressman Mathew Lyon, an Anti-Federalist from Vermont, and numerous government critics were convicted of sedition.

The constitutionality of the Alien and Sedition laws was never actually challenged. The Supreme Court, which in those days heard fewer than a dozen cases a year, never had the opportunity to rule on a sedition case, let alone consider its First Amendment implications. In any case, the furor evaporated when Congress made no move to renew its federal sedition legislation. The Sedition Act expired in 1801 as Thomas Jefferson assumed office as the nation's third president. Yet during the 1798 Sedition Act's short, two-year life span, there were more than two dozen arrests. Nearly a dozen prosecutions resulted in ten convictions for criticism of the government, convictions that tore at the fabric of democratic dissent.[10]

While today we tend to think of freedom of expression and the Constitution as inseparable, First Amendment cases were unknown in the Supreme Court prior to the twentieth century.[11] Judge Thomas Cooley, a highly influential nineteenth-century legal commentator, instructed his readers to "look to the common law for the meaning of freedom of the press." "At the common law," Cooley said, "it will be found that the liberty of the press was neither well protected nor well defined."[12] Professor Timothy Gleason, at the University of Oregon, wrote that even "at the end of the nineteenth century, Alexander Hamilton's common law interpretation of the freedom of the press, put forth in *People v. Croswell*, remained the dominant view of the meaning of freedom of the press: '[Freedom of the press] consists in the right to publish, with impunity, truth, with good motives, for justifiable ends, though reflecting on government, magistrate, or individual.' "[13]

Whatever tolerance for free expression existed among government and the public in eighteenth- and nineteenth-century America, it was qualified by the belief that tolerable speech must be true, carry good motives, and be used for justifiable ends. Few, in government or out, were likely to believe that criticism of national policy carried good motives or justifiable ends.

A Political Menace

More than a century and a quarter passed before Congress again attempted to legislate sedition from the public agenda. Did Congress shy away from more antisedition laws during that long interval because there was no felt need, or because the lawmakers sensed a lack of public support? Whatever the reason, there was no lack of popular fervor for the laws aimed at silencing pacifists and radicals in 1917 and 1918.

The *New York Times* editorialized September 16, 1917, under the headline:

"The Soap Box Preachers of Sedition"

The newspaper called on the governor to do something about "persons guilty of seditious public utterances, commonly spoken of as 'soap box orators,' who in their addresses to street crowds have repeatedly opposed the enforcement of law, attacked the Government and assailed the allies of the United States." After suggesting that officials feared the votes of radicals more than they respected the law, the *Times* editorial concluded that the "heel of authority must crush the heads of the serpents of sedition before they have become too numerous."[14]

The same day the public in Hartford, Connecticut, put life into the *Times'* call for action. Pacifists Annie Riley Hale and Alfred E. Whitehead had a good deal of difficulty finding an auditorium for their rally. After every theater in Hartford refused them admission, the only place available was Socialist Hall. There, representing the

People's Council of America for Democracy and Peace, activists Hale and Whitehead drew a mixed crowd. About half of the audience was sympathetic to the cause. The other half consisted of off duty soldiers and sailors looking for something to do and someone to heckle. When Hale criticized President Wilson and attacked the draft, the hecklers found their target and rushed the stage. Arrests were made. Hale and Whitehead were jailed by local detectives and federal agents who had decided from the outset to let the pacifists speak only in order to gather "evidence" against them.[15] The pair was released from jail two days later and the charges were dropped.[16] If they had not broken the law, they had indeed insulted public sensibilities.

Just as intolerable as sedition was pacifism. Leon Samson, a Columbia University junior, found the university suddenly closed to him in 1917 after he spoke out against the war with Germany. Seeking help from the courts and a mandamus order for readmittance to classes, the judge in Samson's case instead responded that the pacifist was a "political menace to the morals of the student body and a blot on the good name and fame of the honored university whose degree he seeks."[17]

In Cincinnati, Ohio, police were ordered to prevent a public antiwar speech, "Eight-Million Dead." Local halls received the same order from Public Safety Director Friedlander, who vowed that "no meetings that tend to interfere with the avowed purposes of the Government in connection with this war will be permitted in this city."[18]

The New York Times continued its opinion page drive against anyone in disagreement with national policy raising the stakes with demands that agitators lose their civil rights.

> But there is a time when free speech and free action must take heed lest they abuse their privilege. There is a time when, sending its sons to battle, a nation, fighting for paramount rights the vindication of which transcends immeasurably the free play of individual opinion, must be intolerant of opinions that are dangerous. . . . Those who, from whatever cause, take, in effect, the enemy side and strive to thwart the purpose of their country have no more rights here, and are entitled to no more sympathy than if they were active alien enemies.[19]

Examples of both public and governmental intolerance for

speech during the first decades of the twentieth century are easily available.[20] Hundreds of newspapers came under investigation in 1917, suspected of seditious writing.[21] Editors were arrested.[22] Regulations were passed requiring foreign language papers to print translations of everything published.[23] Much of the public cheered. It is natural then that historians, legal scholars, civil libertarians, journalists, and others concerned with the right to speak out have concentrated intensely on the meaning of the *Schenck* decision, the clear and present danger test, and the sedition laws themselves.[24] In a sense, *Schenck* and the sedition prosecutions that followed suggest a kind of David and Goliath courtroom clash between the government and the First Amendment right to speak or publish views outside the mainstream of popular conviction. The fact that when it came to sedition David lost to the governmental Goliath does not lessen our interest in the battle. If anything, it makes it all the more compelling.

Tests, Events, and Constitutions

Two distinct approaches to the World War I sedition cases and the events surrounding them have emerged and account for the bulk of the literature that explores this period of American legal history. In essence, one approach concentrates on the law and the other on the impact of the law.

The legal approach has examined judicial tests and formulas, developed by the courts, which carry names such as the clear and present danger test, the clear and probable danger test, the bad tendency test, and the reasonableness doctrine. The goal in this research approach is to identify exactly where the line—at least from the point of view of the courts—is drawn between legal dissent and speech that is dangerous enough that it may be abridged without violating the First Amendment proscription against abridgment. This line of inquiry traces Supreme Court decisions from 1919 right up to the present. A very short detour to identify the state of sedition cases and the First Amendment shield against them some two hundred years after the ratification of the Bill of Rights is in order.

Antisedition laws, such as the 1940 Smith Act, remain on the books today, although few sedition prosecutions have been attempted since the combination of the cold war with the Soviet Union and the commitment of American troops to combat in Korea stoked the fires of public intolerance during the 1950s. The government did not use the Smith Act or any other antisedition law to prosecute vocal critics of the controversial Vietnam War. Instead, protesters and pacifists found themselves the targets of an odd assortment of federal conspiracy prosecutions and, in some cases, targets of extralegal wiretaps and harassment. The last successful Smith Act prosecution was in 1961.[25] A few other sedition cases have been prosecuted.

In 1969, for example, the Court set a new line marking the boundary between legal and illegal expression. The case involved the First Amendment right of a group of Ku Klux Klansmen to demonstrate in Ohio, where an antisedition statute made it a crime to advocate unlawful acts as a means of political reform. The Supreme Court ruled in *Brandenburg v. Ohio* that the law must distinguish between the mere advocacy of ideas and real incitement to unlawful conduct.[26] Finally putting an end to the clear and present danger test and its progeny as the litmus test for constitutionally permissible abridgments of speech, the Court's per curiam opinion stated that "the constitutional guarantees of free speech and free press do not permit a State to forbid or proscribe advocacy of the use of force or of law violation except where such advocacy is directed to inciting or producing imminent lawless action or is likely to incite or produce such actions."[27] In none of its forms had the clear and present danger test succeeded directly in shielding a speaker from conviction under antisedition legislation. On the fiftieth anniversary of *Schenck* the Court expanded the constitutional protection available to all citizens, even the Klan.

A 1971 case, while usually considered in terms of prior restraint rather than sedition, nonetheless deserves mention. A divided Court ruled 6 to 3 that the *Washington Post* and the *New York Times* could not be restrained from publishing historical documents about American involvement in the war in Vietnam. The government's attempt to prohibit the dissemination of information (sedition normally refers to punishment *after* dissemination) testifies to the continuing nature of the problem of drawing a line between national security and freedom of speech in a democracy. Whether government action occurs as prior restraint or punishment for illegal speech, at least one question remains constant. When does expression lose its constitutional protection? The Court simply ruled, in what came to be known popularly as the Pentagon Papers case, that the government had not met the "heavy burden of proof" required by the First Amendment to justify prior restraint.[28]

The reemergence of sedition and national security issues each decade or so reinforces the need for scrupulous examinations of each new case and the need to understand the origins of the courts' First Amendment approach to them. We want to know what the courts will do. How far can Congress go before the courts will tighten the reigns and pull them back? We also want to know the relationship between the myriad tests and doctrines established by judges interpreting the Constitution and the First Amendment that supplies the rationale for those boundary marking tests. Does the court's operationalization of First Amendment theory each time it is confronted with government repression of expression adequately satisfy the need for unlimited public discussion required to safeguard democratic principles?

Implicit in the body of work focused on judicial tests and doctrines has been the assumption that *Schenck* provides the Supreme Court's first enunciation of the boundaries of First Amendment protection. It does and it does not. In the end defendants Baer and Schenck were jailed. That event alone supports the proposition that the Supreme Court, at least implicitly, set the limit of constitutional protection at the point at which it perceived a clear and present danger to the nation.

It also can be argued, however, that the Court, in *Schenck*, never gave serious, explicit thought to the First Amendment. Instead, the justices considered narrow questions involving the violation of a specific statute—the Espionage Act of 1917 and the Sedition Amendment of 1918. That, in fact, is the primary argument I will offer and defend throughout this discussion. And although it is a line of inquiry that has not been followed in the literature to date, it is a thesis first suggested six decades ago in the *Harvard Law Review*. In his 1919 article, "Freedom of Speech in Wartime," Harvard legal scholar Zechariah Chafee wrote of the *Schenck* case,

> Justice Holmes in his Espionage Act decisions had a magnificent opportunity to make articulate for us that major premise, under which judges ought to classify words as inside or outside the scope of the First Amendment. He, we hoped, would concentrate his great abilities on fixing the line. Instead, like other judges, he has told us that

certain plainly unlawful utterances are, to be sure, unlawful.[29]

The second approach to the Espionage Act and Sedition
Amendment cases is less concerned with legalistic esoterica that might
occupy an attorney or a First Amendment theorist. Here, scholarship
has focused on events and the phenomenon of abridged expression —
federal attempts to suppress minority newspapers,[30] and the denial of
visas to radical noncitizens invited to speak in the United States.[31] It is
an approach of special interest to journalists and civil libertarians
because it documents specific instances of repressive government control. The concern here is not with the law, but with the law's effect.
Speech and political dissent have been abridged. Expression has been
punished. Men and women have been jailed.

Both approaches — the impact of the law and the application of
the law — are necessary elements of any serious understanding of
freedom of expression in the United States. No one approach is sufficient in and of itself. It is reasonable then to posit that much of our
understanding of the origins of twentieth-century, First Amendment
protection may be based on a conceptual flaw that will remain as long
as we continue to assume that Holmes's *Schenck* opinion provides a
substantive, constitutional interpretation. Scholars have considered
the impact of the law and the application of the law, but they have not
considered the process of jurisprudence that underlies these two elements.

Freedom of Speech
v. the First Amendment

The heart of the problem is the temptation to assume
that a situation requiring the Supreme Court to consider freedom of
expression automatically draws into play serious consideration of the
First Amendment. The High Court was aware of the First Amendment in the 1919 sedition cases. Justice Holmes pointed out in *Schenck*
the defendants' contention that they were "protected by the First
Amendment to the Constitution."[32] Judicial references to the First
Amendment do not mean, however, that the First Amendment was
the Court's dominant consideration.

The claim that any given case was in fact decided on First Amendment grounds requires special attention to the Court's decision-making processes. The rules of law the Court applied, how those rules were applied, whether the Court actually relied on the First Amendment to reach its decision, or whether it found alternative, non–First Amendment grounds on which to base its holding must all be considered, even in a situation explicitly involving issues of freedom of expression.

A case decided by the Supreme Court in 1980 illustrates the danger of assuming that free speech issues will always be decided on First Amendment grounds.

Frank Snepp, a former agent in the Central Intelligence Agency, published a book entitled *Decent Interval*.[33] Snepp's popularly selling work detailed the actions of the CIA during the Vietnam War. In essence, the case centered on an employment contract Snepp signed while still working for the intelligence agency. The contract stipulated that Snepp, or any other CIA employee, would not publish any CIA-related information without first submitting the writing to the agency for review and clearance. Snepp published his book without submitting it for prior approval.

The Supreme Court disposed of Snepp's case with a per curiam opinion (an unsigned opinion for which no member of the court takes credit for the writing). Snepp raised First Amendment questions during the trial phase of his case and again when the lower courts held that he would have to turn over all profits on the book to the CIA. Nonetheless, the majority in the Supreme Court saw no First Amendment issue raised by Snepp's skirmish with the government spy agency over the right to publish, and to reap the profits, from a book he had written after leaving its employ. Instead of focusing on freedom of expression, the Court found that Snepp "breached a fiduciary obligation and that the proceeds of his breach are impressed with a constructive trust."[34] Despite Snepp's claim that the government violated his First Amendment rights, and despite the presence of issues clearly rooted within the context of freedom of expression, the Supreme Court reached its conclusion on the basis of ordinary contract law, not on the merits of constitutional counterclaims. A commentator would be free to criticize the Snepp case because it did not give great weight to freedom of expression. But the Snepp Court should not be criticized for its First Amendment interpretations.

There were no First Amendment interpretations, and alternative explanations, such as contract law, are needed to explain what happened.

There is a strong parallel between *Snepp* and free speech or Espionage Act cases such as *Schenck*. In *Schenck* people were arrested, tried, and convicted for expressing themselves in a manner the legislature forbade. Free speech issues were explicitly involved, and *Schenck*, like *Snepp*, has been criticized on First Amendment grounds precisely because of the presence of free speech issues. But is the criticism of *Schenck* based on the same legal fallacy implicit in criticism of *Snepp?* That is, because *Schenck* contained easily identifiable free speech issues, have we assumed too quickly that it was a First Amendment case?

It is easy, at least outside of the courtroom, where procedural rules mandate careful attention to subtle distinctions, to lose sight of the fact that constitutional law and freedom of expression are not necessarily one in the same. Many things that fall under the general category of freedom of expression do not fall within the parameters of issues that raise First Amendment questions that may be settled by a court.

Schenck presented the Court with questions of criminal law as well as issues of freedom of speech. Criticism of *Schenck* as a First Amendment case is too narrow. As with *Snepp*, criticizing the First Amendment elements of *Schenck* without addressing the other points of law that were involved can lead to a distorted view of the role the First Amendment plays in litigation involving freedom of expression. Statutory interpretation, rules of evidence, and traditional, sometimes formalized, procedural restraints on judicial decision making influence the Court at least as heavily as constitutional interpretation. *Schenck* and the Espionage Act cases that followed were important to the development of legal precedent and remain vital to an appreciation of freedom of expression in the United States.[35]

Many critics of Holmes's clear and present danger test bemoan the lack of protection it made available to speakers who found themselves in disagreement with American foreign policy, and they decry the judicial precedent it established. Philosopher and First Amendment theorist Alexander Meiklejohn attacked the Espionage Act cases in 1948. "In [1919] and in the years which have ensued, the Court, following the lead of Justice Oliver Wendell Holmes, has persistently ruled that the freedom of speech of the American community may constitutionally be abridged by legislative action. The ruling annuls the most significant purpose of the First Amendment," Meiklejohn said.[36]

Oregon Supreme Court Justice Hans Linde disapproves not only of Holmes's clear and present danger test, but of the Supreme Court's continued failure to explore the implications of the First Amendment. "Fifty years after the birth of 'clear and present danger,' the Court's position remains ambivalent about the circumstances and the intrinsic content of expression in First Amendment analysis," Linde wrote.[37]

Was *Schenck* an authoritative interpretation of the Constitution or a routine and poorly decided criminal case that has led us astray? Louis Brandeis, an associate justice of the Supreme Court when Holmes wrote the clear and present danger test, later told Justice Felix Frankfurter, "I have never been quite happy about my concurrence in the *Debs* and *Schenck* cases. I had not then thought the issues of freedom of speech out. I thought at the subject, not through it."[38] In and of itself, Brandeis's comment is, of course, inconclusive. Yet Brandeis's admission, and the criticisms of Chafee, Linde, and Meiklejohn demand a reexamination of the judicial reasoning that created the clear and present danger doctrine in 1919. Their statements raise the possibility that there are alternative explanations of the Court's *Schenck* decision that are not grounded in First Amendment jurisprudence.

Where are they? The place to begin is with *Schenck v. United States.* If there is an alternative to the thesis that *Schenck* was decided on First Amendment grounds, it lies in an understanding of the jurisprudence of Justice Holmes, the author of the clear and present danger test. Jurisprudence is a central concept throughout, and it is worth taking the time to define it adequately. A useful and usable structure was provided by Henry Campbell Black. Jurisprudence, Black said, is the "philosophy of law, or the science which treats the principles of positive law and legal relations. In the proper sense of the word, 'jurisprudence' is the science of law, namely, that science which has for its function to ascertain the principles on which legal rules are based, so as not only to classify those rules in their proper order, and show the relation to which they stand to one another, but also to settle the manner in which new or doubtful cases should be brought under the appropriate rules."[39]

Holmes's vision of the law will also provide an understanding of judicial decision making on the Supreme Court, of the historical and institutional influences upon a justice of the High Court, of the factors that may betray our commonsense notions of how the Court comes to justify any given decision, and of the difference between the concept of freedom of expression dear to those lucky enough to live in a democracy and the legal parameters of the First Amendment.

3

Oyez! Oyez! Oyez!

> Year by year the men who had felt their authority in danger had been accumulating lists of immediate enemies . . . Fighting as best they could in the prewar years, groups of these determined citizens then launched a series of brutal, thorough attacks after 1917 against the most vulnerable of the so-called radicals. Through posses, state and Federal prosecutions, and government censorship, they seriously weakened the Socialist party, broke the strength of the International Workers of the World, and stamped out a variety of weaker, fringe activities that ranged from the grumblings of tenant farmers to dissenting little magazines. None of this was done under the shadow of a guilty conscience.
>
> ROBERT WIEBE, 1967,
> *The Search for Order 1877-1920*

J ANUARY 9, 1919, was an important day for Philadelphia attorneys Henry J. Gibbons and Henry John Nelson. They were in Washington, D.C., and their case was listed on the official calendar of the United States Supreme Court as one of ten scheduled for argument that day. Their clients, Dr. Elizabeth Baer and Charles T. Schenck, had received prison sentences for conspiracy to violate the Espionage Act. Unless the attorneys could now convince a majority of the nine-member Bench to overrule the trial court, the sentences would be carried out.

The Supreme Court appeal of the convictions of Baer and Schenck climaxed almost a year and a half of federal action against the two defendants, but even the *New York Times* gave little notice to the first Espionage Act case to reach the High Court. The *Times* simply listed the case in its "Court Calendar" on page eighteen as case numbers 437 and 438.[1] *Times* readers on this day were probably more interested in detailed front-page reports of Theodore Roosevelt's funeral. The former president and Rough Rider was buried the day before in a family plot that overlooked the water across the bay from Roosevelt's Long Island home. The *Times* also reported that West Virginia was the latest state to ratify Congress's prohibition amendment.

Roosevelt's death and prohibition made for good newspaper reading, but Gibbons and Nelson could find news more important to them on the first page of Thursday's *Times*. A headline in column two near the top of the page reported, "Berger Convicted With Four Others."[2] Victor L. Berger was one of the founders of the Socialist party in the United States. He came to America from Austria in 1878 at the age of eighteen. His interest in politics led him to become the first Socialist seated in the United States House of Representatives, where he served one term from 1911 to 1913. Berger again ran for the House in 1918. His bid for the 66th Congress from Milwaukee was successful with the voters, but the House of Representatives refused to seat him because of his public opposition to the war. The newspaper reported that morning that a federal district court trial jury in Chicago convicted the Socialist of violation of the Espionage Act, the same act that formed the basis of the convictions against Baer and Schenck.[3] *Schenck* was the first Espionage Act case to reach the Supreme Court on First Amendment grounds, but it was not an unusual case for the government. The Federal Department of Justice had announced more than twelve hundred cases under the Espionage Act since its passage in 1917.[4]

The Berger conviction story could offer little encouragement to Gibbons and Nelson. The article said the Chicago jury found Berger guilty of sedition and disloyalty under the Espionage Act. The war with Germany was over, but the newspaper reported that the pro-German factor was continuously raised at the trial against the defendants. The government never tried to prove that Berger had direct German funding or aid from the German Imperial government, but, the *Times* reported, "the German influences were constantly brought out."[5] The *Times* said that "Berger was shown to have been born in

Austria."[6] The implication was that the Austrian connection was damning evidence.

Long Live the Constitution
of the United States

John Lord O'Brian was special assistant to the attorney general for war work.[7] He too was ready on January 9 to argue the *Schenck* case before the Supreme Court. O'Brian, together with Alfred Bettman, another special assistant to the attorney general, prepared a thirty-six-page legal brief. In essence, the brief argued that the United States District Court for the Eastern District of Pennsylvania had correctly convicted Baer and Schenck under provisions of the Espionage Act of obstructing the draft.

O'Brian and Bettman sketched a picture of conspiracy between Baer, Schenck, and members of the Socialist party to disrupt the American war effort. The scenario, according to the federal prosecutors, began on a spring day in 1917 when Congress passed the Selective Service Act.[8] By June 30, President Woodrow Wilson ordered the draft regulations into effect and draft boards across the country called men to report for physical examinations and induction into the armed forces. However, conscription did not arouse universal patriotism or blind obedience to the call to military duty. The war in Europe was seen by some, not as a war of ideologies, but rather as the ultimate profit adventure of industrial capitalists that spawned the first American draft since the Civil War. Early on draft opponents challenged conscription as unconstitutional and a form of indentured servitude outlawed by the antislavery clause of the Thirteenth Amendment. The courts acted quickly to quell the legal questions surrounding the draft and within months the Supreme Court ruled that the Selective Service Act was indeed constitutional.[9] Nevertheless, some religious and political groups continued to oppose the draft, and on August 13, 1917, five months before the Court ruled on the constitutionality of conscription, the Socialist party of Philadelphia met to discuss the distribution of an antidraft leaflet.

The Socialist party headquarters in Philadelphia was at 1326 Arch Street. The offices were managed, according to the government, by Charles T. Schenck. Schenck, the party's general secretary, was joined at headquarters on August 13 by other members of the Executive Committee and by Elizabeth Baer. Baer acted as recording secretary for the committee's meeting and took minutes in a small black notebook. Despite government insistence at her trial that Baer was also a member of the Executive Committee, she never admitted to any duplicity or importance within the party beyond her role as notetaker.

The case against Baer and Schenck described the following order of events. At the August 13 meeting Baer's minutes recorded that a motion was moved and seconded "that 15,000 leaflets be written to be printed on the leaflet now in use to be mailed to men who have passed exemption boards, also distribution."[10] The motion was adopted along with another motion that "secretary gets bids on price of leaflets."[11]

The federal prosecutors said that "shortly thereafter, one Lazar went to the printing shop of a newspaper entitled the *Jewish World,* in order to get bids on the circulars."[12] The government's Supreme Court brief included no other information as to who Lazar was (his full name was never given), other than that he was "soliciting business for the *Jewish World.*"[13] The government brief said that Lazar was joined by Schenck, apparently on August 16, when the two men made final printing arrangements at the newspaper printshop.

According to the government, the finished circulars were brought to the Arch Street offices and piled on a table "for free distribution so that anybody who wanted them could come into headquarters and receive them."[14] Clara Abramowitz, who ran the bookshop at the Socialist party offices, later told federal officials that "in pursuance of defendant Schenck's direction, [she] gave the circulars to all who called and asked for them."[15] Abramowitz told authorities that Schenck also instructed her to give out stamped envelopes to any who wanted them. The prosecutors said the envelopes were intended for use in distributing the circulars and cited the minutes of an August 20 Executive Committee session that stated, "Comrade Schenck be authorized to spend $125 for sending letters through the mail."[16]

There is no record of how many leaflets were actually distributed or of the public's reaction to reading the antidraft material. It is clear, however, that the government took notice. Federal officers appeared August 28 at the Arch Street headquarters and entered with a search warrant and a warrant for Schenck's arrest. Inside Schenck's offices the federal officers found and seized "the minute book, bundles of the circulars, and many newspaper clippings containing lists of the names and addresses of the men who had been accepted for military service by the draft boards."[17]

The contraband circulars consisted of single sheets of paper with a message on each side. The first side bore the title, "Long Live the Constitution of the United States. Wake Up, America. Your Liberties are in Danger." The text argued forcefully against the draft and stated that those in agreement should "join the Socialist Party in its campaign for the repeal of the conscription act."[18] O'Brian and Bettman introduced the following excerpts into evidence:

> A conscript is little better than a convict. He is deprived of his liberty and of his right to think and act as a free man. A conscripted citizen is forced to surrender his right as a citizen and become a subject. He is forced into involuntary servitude. He is deprived of the protection given him by the Constitution of the United States. He is deprived of all freedom of conscience in being forced to kill against his will. Are you one who is opposed to war, and were you misled by the venal capitalist newspapers or intimidated or deceived by gang politicians and registrars into believing that you would not be allowed to register your objection to conscription? Do you know that many citizens of Philadelphia insisted on their right to answer the famous question twelve, and went on record with their honest opinion of opposition to war, notwithstanding the deceitful efforts of our rulers and the newspaper press to prevent them from doing so? Shall it be said that the citizens of Philadelphia, the cradle of American liberty, are so lost to a sense of right and justice that they will let such monstrous wrongs against humanity go unchallenged? Conscription laws belong to a bygone age. Even the people of Germany, long suffering under the yoke of militarism, are beginning to demand the abolition of conscription. Do you think it has a place in the United States? Do you want to see unlimited power handed over to Wall Street's chosen few in America? If you do not, join the Socialist Party in its campaign for the repeal of the conscription act.

The reverse side of the circular again opposed the draft and warned of the "Moloch of Militarism."[19]

ASSERT YOUR RIGHTS

The Socialist Party says that any individual or officers of the law intrusted with the administration of conscription regulations violate the provisions of the United States Constitution, the supreme law of the land, when they refuse to recognize your right to assert your opposition to the draft.

In exempting clergymen and members of the Society of Friends (popularly called Quakers) from active military service the examination boards have discriminated against you.

If you do not assert and support your rights you are helping to "deny or disparage rights" which it is the solemn duty of all citizens and residents of the United States to retain.

In lending tacit or silent consent to the conscription law, in neglecting to assert your rights, you are (whether knowingly or not) helping to condone and support a most infamous and insidious conspiracy to abridge and destroy the sacred and cherished rights of a free people. You are a citizen: not a subject! You delegate your power to the officers of the law to be used for your good and welfare, not against you.

They are your servants; not your masters. Their wages come from the expenses of government which you pay. Will you allow them to unjustly rule you?

No power was delegated to send our citizens away to foreign shores to shoot up the people of other lands, no matter what may be their internal or international disputes.

To draw this country into the horrors of the present war in Europe, to force the youth of our land into the shambles and bloody trenches of war-crazy nations, would be a crime the magnitude of which defies description. Words could not express the condemnation such cold-blooded ruthlessness deserves.

Will you stand idly by and see the Moloch of Militarism reach forth across the sea and fasten its tentacles upon this continent? Are you willing to submit to the degradation of having the Constitution of the United States treated as a "mere scrap of paper"?

No specious or plausible pleas about a "war for de-

mocracy" can becloud the issue. Democracy can not be
shot into a nation. It must come spontaneously and purely
from within.

Democracy must come through liberal education.
Upholders of military ideas are unfit teachers.

To advocate the persecution of other peoples through
the prosecution of war is an insult to every good and
wholesome American tradition.

You are responsible. You must do your share to
maintain, support, and uphold the rights of the people of
this country.

In this world crisis where do you stand? Are you
with the forces of liberty and light or war and darkness?

Taken as a whole, the government argued, the circular was
intended to obstruct the draft.

The federal raid on the Philadelphia headquarters resulted on
September 15, 1917, in indictments against William J. Higgins, Jacob H. Root, Charles Sehl, and Baer and Schenck. All five were tried
for violation of the Espionage Act. The government produced ten
witnesses at the trial identified as "registrants under the Selective
Service Law who had been examined and accepted by the draft
boards."[20] In a dramatic move, some of the witnesses opened on the
stand letters addressed to them containing the circulars in question.
When the defense and prosecution rested their cases, the trial judge
instructed the jury to find Higgins, Root, and Sehl not guilty of
obstructing the draft and to consider only the evidence against Baer
and Schenck. He said there was not enough evidence against the
other three to sustain a conviction. The jury found Baer and Schenck
guilty and the judge denied a defense motion for a new trial.

An Intelligible Moment
of the Unintelligible

Oliver Wendell Holmes, Jr., was seventy-eight years
old when the *Schenck* case reached the Supreme Court. He was appointed to the Court in 1902 by President Theodore Roosevelt and he
came to the Bench with a strong reputation in legal circles that was
established by nearly twenty years on the Supreme Judicial Court of

Massachusetts and dramatized by the publication of his best-known writing, *The Common Law,* in 1881.[21] Holmes served on the Massachusetts bench as an associate justice from 1822 to 1899 and as chief justice from 1899 to 1901. The state court provided the opportunity to develop a strong sense of the judicial role in common law and statutory law, but provided far less occasion to consider legal issues radiating from the Federal Constitution.

The associate justice rarely read the newspapers. He preferred to spend his hours away from the Court's business writing letters and reading literature and philosophy. In a typical exchange just before the United States Supreme Court's 1918 Christmas recess, Holmes reported to his friend, Sir Frederick Pollock, a brief encounter with a book on mysticism in English literature. "The theme interests me," Holmes wrote. "I am a mystic in the sense of believing myself to be an intelligible moment of the unintelligible."[22] Holmes professed less interest in current events and politics.

Holmes did not know he would write the *Schenck* decision when the justices robed for the Court's January 9 session. Such assignments come only after a case is argued and a preliminary conference and vote is held among the nine justices. When the chief justice is a member of the majority, he may either write the opinion or assign its writing to another. If the chief justice does not vote with the majority, the senior associate justice voting with the majority selects the justice who will write the opinion.

The robing ceremony was part of a long tradition by the time the justices met to hear *Schenck.* They gathered in the robing room to don their black judicial robes and to shake hands, but one justice broke the pattern. James C. McReynolds was cordial to six of his colleagues, but he showed open hostility toward Justices Louis D. Brandeis and John H. Clarke. Born in Elkton, Kentucky in 1862, McReynolds was appointed to the Court by President Woodrow Wilson in 1914. He sometimes refused altogether to speak to Clarke, whom he considered to be "stupid," and, as a confirmed anti-Semite, McReynolds went through long periods of giving a cold shoulder to Brandeis, the only Jewish member of the Court.[23]

The nine justices filed into the courtroom in a straight line. Attorneys Gibbons, Nelson and O'Brian rose to their feet with everyone else in the room as Marshall Frank K. Green voiced the traditional chant, "Oyez! Oyez! Oyez! All persons having business before

the Honorable, the Supreme Court of the United States, are ad-
monished to draw near and give their attention, for the Court is now
sitting. God save the United States and this Honorable Court!" There
was a long straight wooden bench at the head of the room behind
which the justices sat to either side of Chief Justice Edward Douglas
White. High on the wall above White's high-backed leather chair was
a round-faced clock. There was also a red, white, and blue shield with
twenty-six stars. It dated back to John Quincy Adams's presidency.
The courtroom itself was the old Senate Chamber in the Capitol
Building, first turned over to the Court in 1860.

Besides Brandeis, Clarke, Holmes, McReynolds, and White,
the 1919 Court included Justices William Rufus Day, James Mc-
Kenna, Mahlon Pitney, and Willis Van Devanter. Like Holmes, Day
was appointed to the Court by Theodore Roosevelt. Van Devanter
and Pitney were appointed by William Howard Taft. James Mc-
Kenna, the senior associate justice, was appointed to the Court in
1898 by William McKinley. Each justice, including the chief justice,
had an equal vote.

4

The Case Before the Court

On the one side are those who contend that liberty of discussion has not been violated by the Espionage Act cases and state sedition prosecutions. Just as Blackstone defended the suppressions of his time by saying that freedom of speech was preserved years before when the censorship had been abolished, so the conservatives today insist that it was made sufficiently secure a century ago when juries were given control of sedition prosecutions.

ZECHARIAH CHAFEE, 1941,
Free Speech in the United States

The Plaintiffs-in-Error

Attorneys Gibbons and Nelson began their oral arguments before the Supreme Court on January 9, 1919.[1] They introduced no new witnesses or physical evidence. The Supreme Court does not consider new evidence or testimony. The job of ascertaining facts is left to the trial court jury and the justices will not second-guess jurors. Supreme Court justices decide whether the appropriate law was applied and whether that law was applied correctly. The High Court may also consider whether the lower court followed the proper procedures. In all cases, however, the Court is limited to consideration of legal arguments raised by the appellants. The Court can and does ask questions during oral argument. But the Court cannot decide a case based on rules of law not previously argued.

The trial court had found Baer and Schenck guilty of three crimes. The first was conspiracy to violate Section 4, Title I, of the Espionage Act, which stated that:

Whoever, when the United States is at war, shall wilfully cause or attempt to cause insubordination, disloyalty, mutiny or refusal of duty in the military or naval forces of the United States, or shall wilfully obstruct the recruiting or enlistment service of the United States, to the injury of the service or of the United States, shall be punished by a fine of not more than $10,000, or imprisonment for not more than twenty years, or both.[2]

Baer and Schenck were also found guilty "of conspiracy to commit an offense against the United States—that is, the use of the mails for the transmission of matter (circulars) declared by Section 2, Title XII, of the Act to be non-mailable." Finally, the trial court found the pair guilty of "the use of the mails for the transmission of such matter."[3]

Attorneys Gibbons and Nelson raised three primary questions for the Court. They asked the justices to consider whether the Espionage Act "constitutes an abridgment of freedom of speech and the right of petition in contravention of the First Amendment to the Constitution," and they asked the Court to consider whether Baer and Schenck "were lawfully found guilty of conspiracy under all the evidence."[4] Finally, the attorneys asked "whether or not papers seized under a search warrant were lawfully used as evidence against them under the constitutional provision against unlawful search (Amendment IV of the Constitution), and the constitutional provision against a defendant being made to testify against himself (Amendment V of the Constitution)."[5]

Gibbons and Nelson were trying to construct a two-tiered defense for Baer and Schenck. The first level struck at the basic constitutional issue of freedom of speech. The second level of defense challenged the technical aspects of the application of the law in their case; that is, was the legal definition of conspiracy properly applied by the lower courts? Did the procedures used by the government for gathering and presenting evidence constitute a technical violation of the defendants' constitutional rights?

Gibbons and Nelson began their challenge with an attack on the antispeech implications of the Espionage Act and a summary of the rationale for freedom of speech. The act, the attorneys said, created three new offenses. Title I, Section 3, made it illegal (1) to make "false statements or reports interfering with military or naval operations or promoting the success of our enemies; (2) [for] causing or attempting to cause insubordination, disloyalty, mutiny or refusal of duty in the military and naval forces; [and] (3) [for] obstruction of enlistment and recruiting."[6]

The defense attempted to show the importance of the First Amendment, its legislative history, and prior cases that supported their arguments, and finally suggested a judicial test they hoped the Court would use to decide the case.

With few exceptions, the attorneys said, American courts followed the doctrine that the First Amendment was intended to prevent the government from censoring information prior to its release. The government could, however, punish individuals for certain types of utterances after they were spoken or written. The thesis that most prior restraints are forbidden by the First Amendment, while post-publication punishments are not, finds support from Holmes, himself. Justice Holmes wrote in a 1907 decision that the "main purpose of the First Amendment is to 'prevent all such previous restraints upon publications as had been practiced by other governments,' and they do not prevent the subsequent punishment of such as may be deemed contrary to the public welfare."[7]

The Espionage Act, Gibbons and Nelson admitted, was based on just such a doctrine. But then, the attorneys continued, "How can a speaker or writer be said to be free to discuss the actions of Government if twenty years in prison stares him in the face if he makes a mistake and says too much? Severe punishment for sedition will stop political discussion as effectively as censorship."[8]

Gibbons and Nelson conceded that the First Amendment gave no protection to the man who violated the draft law by refusing to do military service, "but [the First Amendment] does mean," they argued, that a man "can say the Draft Law is wrong and ought to be repealed."[9]

To Gibbons and Nelson the question was not whether Baer and Schenck put their feelings about the draft into print. The issue was larger. "If all opponents of war are suppressed," the attorneys argued in their brief, "and all advocates of a war are given free rein, is it not conceivable that a peace-loving president might be prevented from making an early, honorable peace, founded on justice!"[10] Gibbons and Nelson asked the Court, "How can the citizens find out whether a war is just or unjust unless there is a free and full discussion!"[11]

The defense brief teetered on a line between two distinct types of First Amendment theory: one dealing with prior restraint, the other with sedition. They were on safe ground arguing against prior restraint. There was a history of strong philosophical and legal opposition to prior restraint in the United States.[12] But their own arguments made it clear that this was not a case of prior restraint. The defendants were being punished after the fact. They were never prevented from speaking.

The attorneys wanted to show that there also was historical support for the contention that the First Amendment was not limited to prohibiting prior restraints upon speech. "When Congress passed the Sedition Law of 1798, punishing 'writings against the United States and the President,' Jefferson treated it as unconstitutional. A few years later Hamilton defended an editor from prosecution," Gibbons and Nelson said.[13]

"The spread of truth in matters of general concern," they continued, "is essential to the stability of a republic. How can truth survive if force is to be used, possibly on the wrong side? Absolutely unlimited discussion is the only means by which to make sure that 'truth is mighty and will prevail.' "[14]

The defense wanted the Supreme Court to accept the notion that First Amendment protection extends to prohibiting punishment even after the dissemination of speech, and they cited more than a half-dozen cases as authority.

For example, the attorneys told the Court, *United States v. Hall* involved a defendant charged with crimes identical to those leveled against their own clients. But in that case, Federal Judge Bourquin ruled, "The Espionage Act is not intended to suppress criticism or denunciation, truth or slander, oratory or gossip, argument or loose talk, but only false facts wilfully put forward as true and broadly, with the specific intent to interfere with army or navy operations."[15] Gibbons and Nelson were trying to show that other courts had already interpreted the meaning of the First Amendment and its relation to the Espionage Act in a manner favorable to their own case.

Finally, Gibbons and Nelson suggested their own "test" to determine when speech surpassed the protection of the First Amendment. "The fair test of protection by the constitutional guarantee of free speech is whether an expression is made with sincere purpose to communicate honest opinion or belief, or whether it masks a primary intent to incite to forbidden action, or whether it does, in fact, incite to forbidden action."[16]

The defense hoped the use of such a test would exonerate their clients. Baer and Schenck, the attorneys said, could hardly be said to have attempted to incite anyone to illegal action. "In fact," they said, "readers were urged to go to the Socialist Party Headquarters . . . and *sign a petition to repeal the Conscription Act*."[17]

The second level of the appeal for Baer and Schenck developed along a more technical reading of the law. In essence, Gibbons and Nelson tried to convince the Supreme Court of two things. First, the attorneys said that although their clients were convicted of conspiracy, the trial court misused the legal definition of conspiracy. Second, the attorneys argued, the evidence used during the trial was not legally admissible in a court of law. Therefore, the judge should have dismissed the charges against the defendants.

Gibbons and Nelson defined a conspiracy as "a criminal agreement on the part of defendants."[18] And a conviction for conspiracy, the attorneys said, "can only be sustained . . . upon positive proof beyond a reasonable doubt of [each defendant's] actual participation in such conspiracy."[19] The attorneys cited five examples of federal case law and one state court ruling to support their argument. The settled rule of law, they said, was that mere knowledge of an alleged conspiracy was "entirely insufficient to sustain a conviction of conspiracy."[20]

Then how could Baer be guilty of conspiracy, her attorneys asked the Court. "The sole testimony against her is that she wrote the minutes of the meeting of the Executive Committee of the Socialist Party dated respectively August 13th and 20th, 1917."[21] Gibbons and Nelson argued that there was no proof that Baer was a member of the Executive Committee, that she voted in favor of the resolution to write and distribute antidraft leaflets noted in her minutes, or, for that matter, that the leaflets found in party headquarters were even the same ones described in the minutes. Yet the Socialists' lawyers concluded, the "indictment charges the defendants . . . with having committed the said acts 'as members of the Executive Committee of the Socialist Party.' "[22]

The wording was important because "the alleged crime of which . . . Schenck was found guilty . . . is the crime of conspiracy which is inevitably predicated upon the acts and criminal cooperation of at least two persons."[23] Under that technical reading of the law, "the conviction against defendant Schenck can not stand unless a criminal agreement between him and the Executive Committee of the Socialist Party was shown."[24] All that was shown against Schenck, the lawyers said, was that he ordered the circular in question and kept copies of it in his office. In itself, that was not a criminal conspiracy. The attorneys said the key question, then, was: "Is there in the testimony herein any legal, admissible proof of any agreement, understanding, co-operation or connection between [Schenck] and the Executive Committee of the Socialist Party in the drafting, planning, printing, circulating, distributing or mailing of the said leaflets or circulars?"[25] The defense counsel claimed there was no such proof. Schenck was wrongly convicted. A criminal conspiracy was not shown.

There was also a question of the admissibility of the government evidence against Schenck. Again citing case law, defense counsel said that while the minutes might be used against Baer, they were not legally admissible as evidence against Schenck. "In a criminal prosecution acts and declarations of one conspirator made in the absence and beyond the hearing of an alleged co-conspirator, are not admissible against the latter."[26]

Finally, the attorneys said there was no proof to uphold the third count against Schenck — that he had used the mails in violation of the Espionage Act. "The record is barren," the attorneys said, "of any proof that the defendant Schenck mailed or attempted to mail a single one of such circulars."[27] Gibbons and Nelson said the alleged appropriation of $125 by the Executive Committee for mailing costs was not admissible evidence. Counsel for Baer and Schenck rested their case with three final arguments.

The Fourth Amendment to the Constitution governs the use of search warrants. It states in part that "no warrants shall issue, but upon probable cause, supported by oath." Gibbons and Nelson said that the evidence against their clients was obtained with a search warrant to go through the Socialist party headquarters on Arch Street. But, the warrant was issued by the attorney general on the testimony of a post office inspector who "failed to show how it was he got his belief, and why he did believe" the Socialist offices needed to be searched.[28] In other words, there was no showing of probable cause when the warrant was issued. Without that showing, the warrant was illegal and any evidence obtained under an illegal warrant could not be used in court. The attorneys cited four examples of case law to support their contention.[29]

The Fifth Amendment to the Constitution states, "No person shall be compelled . . . in any criminal case to be a witness against himself." Gibbons and Nelson suggested that the Court should interpret this to mean that not only was the government barred from forcing Schenck to testify against himself, it was also prohibited from introducing papers written by Schenck as evidence. "The Constitution was intended," Schenck's attorneys said, "to prevent a prosecutor from making a defendant testify against himself, whether by verbal, written, printed or other testimony."[30]

With the legal aspects of their arguments completed, Gibbons and Nelson appealed to the conscience of the Court. "The defendants contend that they are not criminals in the ordinary sense of the word. There is no question of moral turpitude. This is a political question. No matter what the law may be, no matter what even this high Court may decide, there is a question here of human freedom which will not down [sic] in spite of what the laws may say or what the laws may be."[31]

The Case Against Baer and Schenck

John Lord O'Brian, special assistant to the attorney general for war work, worked with Alfred Bettman to prepare a government brief that would answer their adversaries' contentions point by point. Bettman was special assistant to the U.S. attorney general in charge of sedition prosecutions, but he did not appear with O'Brian to present oral arguments.

Gibbons and Nelson had challenged the constitutionality of the Espionage Act as a violation of First Amendment guarantees of freedom of speech. The government responded that there was no inherent attack in the act on freedom of speech. "In substance," the government said, "the defendants were charged with attempting to induce young men subject to the draft law to disobey the requirements of that law."[32] That was not speech, but action. "The intent of the defendants was to influence the conduct of persons subject to the draft and to influence that conduct in relation to the draft."[33] O'Brian and Bettman said the act did not prohibit speech and the defendants were not prosecuted for "legitimate political agitation for the repeal of the draft law."[34] Any such claim, according to the government, was defeated by the fact the defendants sent their circulars to men already drafted. In other words, speech only came into the picture in the sense that it was used as a vehicle to commit a "crime." In this case, the defendants' crime was attempting to "wilfully obstruct the recruiting or enlistment service of the United States" while the country was at war. True, the First Amendment protected speech. But the Espionage Act only prohibited conduct. It did not prohibit speech that was not essentially conduct. The act of speaking or writing was only peripheral to the actual crime.

The government appeared to have little problem countering the case law cited by Gibbons and Nelson. First of all, the government said, none of the cases cited by the defendants held "Section 3 of Title I of the Espionage Act or any part thereof to be unconstitutional."[35] Nor did any of those cases present a substantive challenge to the convictions of Baer and Schenck. O'Brian and Bettman said that the case law cited by the defendants' attorneys was taken out of context. The reference to *Hall,* for example, did not parallel the present facts and, therefore, *Hall* did "not decide any of the questions involved in the instant case."[36]

The defendants' reference to *U.S. v. Ramp* was also a bad choice, the government said.[37] The defense had cited *Ramp* providing the following passage from the opinion:

> A citizen is entitled to fairly criticize men and measure . . . this was a view, by the use of lawful means, to improve the public service, or to amend the laws by which he is governed or to which he is subjected. But when his criticism extends, or leads by wilful intent, to the incitement of disorder or riot, or to the infraction of the laws . . . it overleaps the bounds of all reasonable liberty accorded to him by the guarantee of freedom of speech, and this because the very means adopted is an unlawful exercise of the privilege.[38]

In fact, *Ramp* "clearly support[ed] the Government's contention in the present case, and the remainder of the opinions in those cases

would be found even more advantageous to these contentions."[39] Bettman and O'Brian then provided a long passage from the charge to the
jury in *Ramp* "defining the scope of the constitutional guarantee of free
speech."[40]

> A citizen may not use his tongue or pen in such a way as
> to inflict legal injury upon his neighbor or use his own
> property to the detriment or injury of another. Nor has
> any person the right, under the guaranty of freedom of
> speech, to shape his language in such a way as to incite
> disorder, riot, or rebellion, because such action leads to a
> breach of the peace and disturbs good order and quietude
> in the community. Nor is he privileged to utter such lan-
> guage and sentiment as will lead to an infraction of law,
> for the laws of the land are designed to be observed and
> not to be disregarded and overridden. Much less has he
> the privilege, no matter upon what claim or pretense, so to
> express himself with willful purpose as to lead to the ob-
> struction and resistance of the due execution of the laws of
> the country, or as will induce others to do so.[41]

The government attorneys closed their First Amendment coun-
terarguments by suggesting that, in the end, there was no real question involving a violation of First Amendment rights. They argued
that, inherently, "the Congress of the United States has a constitutional right to prohibit a person from attempting during war to induce
violations of a statute providing for military service."[42]

O'Brian and Bettman turned from First Amendment considerations to the defense claim that Baer's minutes were inadmissible as
evidence against Schenck. They spent little time attacking the claim
and simply pointed out that "the question is not important in this
case, for Schenck himself identified these minutes."[43]

The defense had said that there was a complete lack of evidence
to tie Schenck in with a conspiracy, but the government responded
that, even ignoring Baer's minutes, there was more than enough
evidence to convict Schenck. O'Brian and Bettman said it was clear
that Schenck ordered the seditious leaflets and directed their distribution. Witnesses had testified to that. Lists of draftees were found in
Schenck's files and many of the names corresponded to the draftees
who received the Socialists' leaflets. And, the government said, unidentified people also came to the Socialist party headquarters to pick

up Schenck's circulars. Even if they had not been named or indicted, they were also conspirators. "At least from the time [Schenck] obtained bids for the printing up to the time of his arrest," the government said, "he was an active, in fact the most active, participant in the conspiracy."[44] After citing case law to lend support for their definition of a conspirator, O'Brian and Bettman said that it was "well settled that a man who joins a conspiracy by taking any part in the execution thereof is treated by the law as a co-conspirator."[45]

The government's next rebuttal attacked the defense contention that there was insufficient evidence against Baer to have submitted her case to a jury. The defense claimed the trial judge should have directed for an acquittal. But the government dismissed that contention, stating that Baer was charged with conspiracy and that a conspiracy in which she took part had been shown. The conspiracy consisted of the members of the Socialist party Executive Committee and unidentified persons who aided with the distribution of the leaflets. "As testified by one of her attorneys, Mr. Nelson," the government said, "Dr. Baer was a member of the Executive Committee. She was also the recording secretary of the organization."[46] Her duties as a secretary were damning evidence, according to O'Brian and Bettman. "The recording of these official minutes," they said, "was an essential part of the conspiracy. The defendant Baer herself admitted that the minutes . . . were in her handwriting."[47] The government attorneys admitted that some of the evidence connecting Baer with the conspiracy was circumstantial, but rejoined that "proof of a conspiracy generally is of a circumstantial character."[48] The government had no doubt that the actions of the Executive Committee constituted a conspiracy to violate the Espionage Act and that an individual became a conspirator "by entering into a conspiracy already formed and [hence] becomes responsible for the acts of the other conspirators."[49]

The government attorneys turned the defense counsels' own brief against them to counter the last contention of error. The defense claimed that certain evidence used at the trial violated Fourth Amendment rules regarding search warrants and Fifth Amendment rules applicable to self-incrimination. O'Brian and Bettman pointed out, however, the defense admission that settled case law showed the rule to be that "evidence obtained by means of a search warrant is not inadmissible, either on the ground that it is in the nature of admissions made under duress, or that it is evidence which the defendant has been compelled to furnish against himself."[50] The defense did not like the law as it stood and suggested that the Court should apply a more liberal interpretation to the Constitution than had been done in the past. But, O'Brian and Bettman said, "The constitutional point having, as admitted by them, being settled against the defendants by the [past] decisions of this court, [it] is obviously too unsubstantial and frivolous upon which to predicate the jurisdiction of this court."[51]

Deciding the Case

The oral arguments for Schenck were completed January 10, 1919. Now the Court had to decide whether to uphold the jury's verdict. The formal decision-making procedure was conducted at a judicial conference, a formal meeting of all nine justices.

Chief Justice Edward D. White chaired the meeting, which, like all Supreme Court conferences, was held in secret.[52] Not even a secretary, stenographer or law clerk was allowed into the room to witness the deliberations. If the justices needed something from outside, or if a message arrived, it was up to the junior member of the Bench, Justice John Clarke, to leave the room and accomplish the necessary task. No official records were kept of the justices' deliberations.

The first order of business was a discussion of the case, and every justice who wished was given time to share his thinking on the matter. The traditions of the Court mandated complete courtesy among the justices, and, while each held an equal vote, seniority determined the order in which they would speak, beginning with the chief justice. Interruptions were rare. When all views on the case were heard, Chief Justice White called for a vote. The justices voted one by one, Justice Clarke casting the first vote and Justice White the last. Although there is no formal rule, it is the custom of the Court to allow the justice with the least seniority to vote first and to continue this pattern with the chief justice voting last. In theory, such an arrangement prevents justices with less seniority from being overly influenced by their colleagues.

The vote against Baer and Schenck was unanimous. All nine justices affirmed the lower court decision. The evidence was sufficient to find Baer and Schenck guilty of conspiracy to violate the Espionage Act. The act itself did not violate the right to freedom of speech guaranteed by the First Amendment.

Chief Justice White asked Justice Holmes to write the opinion of the Court. No record was kept of how the justices reached their unanimous decision, of what the justices said in conference, or of whether there were any misgivings within the conference. But Justice Holmes's written opinion provided the Court's legal reasoning to other American judicial bodies and to the public.

At the very least, the justices had a number of elements at their disposal when they met in conference. There was the record of the trial. The written briefs prepared by Gibbons and Nelson, and Bettman and O'Brian, had been distributed to each member of the Bench with sufficient time to read them before oral arguments. In the briefs and during oral arguments the government and defense attorneys presented what they saw as the most important considerations for the Court. The justices had the relevant portions of the Constitution and the Espionage Act. And finally, there were the decisions of past cases that might clarify an applicable rule of law.

But how was the decision made? What did the justices take into account when they cast their votes, and what did Justice Holmes consider when he wrote the Court's opinion? Twenty-eight years earlier Justice Holmes wrote in *The Common Law* that "the life of the law has not been logic: it has been experience. The felt necessities of the time, prevalent moral and political theories, institutions of public policy . . . have had a great deal more to do than the syllogism in determining the rules by which men should be governed. The law embodies the story of a nation's development through many centuries."[53]

Holmes's treatise was philosophical, but it was also meant to provide an understanding of the law. Holmes pointed out several forces at work on the formulation and application of law: "the felt necessities of the time, moral and political theories, institutions of public policy." How much did each of these elements, and others, contribute to and affect the judicial decision-making process? How far do they go toward explaining the Court's decision in the Baer and Schenck Espionage Act case?

Schenck has always been of interest to people concerned about freedom of speech. An individual's right to criticize the government appears to be an integral part of the case. But was the moral and philosophical free speech issue important to the justices who decided the defendants' appeals? Did the justices believe that they were deciding what has come to be known today as a First Amendment case? Twenty-two years before *Schenck*, Holmes wrote, "One of the many evil effects of the confusion between legal and moral ideas . . . is that theory is apt to get the cart before the horse, and to consider the right or the duty as something existing apart from and independent of the consequences of its breach, to which certain sanctions are added afterward."[54]

Justice Holmes's writing suggests that people at times forget that the Court must consider law rather than morals when it decides a case. Applied to *Schenck*, the Court had to consider far more than a philosophy of freedom of speech. In order to understand the Court's decision, then, it is necessary to understand all of the forces that influenced the justices and to give special attention to the differences "between legal and moral ideas," and the possibility that certain "experiences" were just as important to the judicial process as was the "logic" of the law.

5
Judicial Decision Making

Civil liberties draw at best only limited strength from legal guarantees. Preoccupation by our people with the constitutionality, instead of with the wisdom, of legislation or of executive action is preoccupation with a false value. . . . Focusing attention on constitutionality tends to make constitutionality synonymous with wisdom. When legislation touches freedom of thought and freedom of speech, such a tendency is a formidable enemy of a free spirit. . . . The ultimate reliance for the deepest needs of civilization must be found outside their vindication in courts of law; apart from all else, judges, howsoever they may conscienciously seek to discipline themselves against it, unconsciously are too apt to be moved by the deep undercurrents of public feeling.

JUSTICE FELIX FRANKFURTER, 1951,
Dennis v. United States

MERICAN law is both very new and very old. Legal historian Lawrence Friedman wrote in 1972 that, "while one lawyer is advising his client how to react to a ruling from Washington, issued that very day, another may be telling his client that some plausible course of action is blocked by a statute well known to the lawyers of Henry VIII or by decisions of some older judges whose names, language and habits would be unfathomable mysteries to both attorney and client."[1]

Schenck v. United States placed a new law into the Supreme Court arena.[2] The justices had never before ruled on a claim that the Espionage Act violated First Amendment guarantees of freedom of speech. Yet despite the Court's inexperience with the two-year-old statute and despite the unique set of facts the case provided, guidance was available from the past. General principles governed the judicial process and gave specific direction to each justice's conception of the judicial role. In turn, the accepted axioms of the judicial role influenced the Court's decision-making procedures.

Legal principles and doctrines derived from the Constitution, from precedent established in earlier but factually dissimilar cases, and from the traditions of the Court itself identified and defined the judicial methods available to the justices in *Schenck* and ensured that the interpretation and application of even a new law would be consistent with long-accepted practices of the judiciary. The conceptual framework that enabled the justices to develop general legal principles applicable to divergent cases is called jurisprudence, a term that refers to the science and philosophy of law. It is to the elements of jurisprudence that influenced Justice Holmes's opinion in *Schenck* that we will now turn.

Holmes's legal reasoning and his interpretation of the Espionage Act, the law under which Baer and Schenck were convicted, can be found in his written opinion for the Court. The legal principles that guided Holmes's decision-making procedures, however, were established axioms for the Court long before President Woodrow Wilson signed the Espionage Act into law in 1917.

The next step toward an understanding of Holmes's position in *Schenck* is to establish and review some of the axioms of decision making on the Supreme Court. Legal scholar Henry Abraham has described those axioms as an important code of judicial conduct. "Throughout the almost two centuries of its existence," Abraham said, "the Court has developed a host of unwritten laws, practices, precedents, and attitudes which we may well view as a code of behavior for the highest judicial body in the United States."[3]

The Role of the Court

MARBURY v. MADISON. The role of the Supreme Court was ill-defined prior to John Marshall's tenure as Chief Justice of the United States. The Constitution established the

Supreme Court and provided a broad outline of this jurisdiction.[4] The framers went into no detail about the decision-making procedures the Court was to use. *Marbury v. Madison,* argued before the Court in December 1801, provided dramatic clarification of the judicial role and the political considerations inherent in judicial decision making. It took Marshall nearly fourteen months to prepare the final ruling in *Marbury.*[5] When the Chief Justice finally presented the Court's opinion on February 24, 1803, he gave credibility to a controversial legal doctrine called judicial review and, in doing so, established a major role for the Supreme Court in America's infant experiment with self-government.[6]

Marshall's handling of the case demonstrated an element of political theory that has remained a vital component of American jurisprudence. When the Supreme Court acts, it must do more than settle a legal dispute. The Court must also demonstrate that its actions are a legitimate use of judicial power consistent with the separation of powers outlined in the Constitution.[7]

William Marbury's case came to the Court wrapped in political machinations. The Court itself had limited experience and precedent from which to work. Marshall's predecessors produced only fifty-five decisions from the Court's first term in February 1790, to 1801. Even during Marshall's tenure, which lasted until 1835, the Court found no need to hold session more than six weeks a year. But prepared or not, the Court was presented with complicated issues by Marbury's case.

When Thomas Jefferson defeated Federalist party candidate John Adams's bid for reelection in 1800, the lame duck president filled dozens of minor political posts with Federalist appointments in his final weeks. Adams also made a major appointment. The vacancy for Chief Justice of the United States went to Adams's secretary of state, John Marshall.

Marshall accepted the appointment, but he had literally last-minute work to do as Adams's secretary of state. Marshall's final duty for Adams was to affix the Great Seal of the United States to appointments Adams was signing on his last night in office and to see that the commissions were delivered. A commission appointing William Marbury justice of the peace was signed and sealed, but an oversight left it undelivered—the final step necessary to make the appointment official.

Thomas Jefferson became the first president to be inaugurated in

Washington, D.C. The Oath of Office was administered by the new chief justice, John Marshall. Soon afterwards, Jefferson discovered Adams's plot to fill the judiciary with men hostile to his Democratic-Republicans. Furious, Jefferson commanded that none of the undelivered commissions, Marbury's among them, would be served. Marbury sued Jefferson's new secretary of state, James Madison, and asked the Supreme Court to force Madison to make good on the appointment.

Chief Justice John Marshall ruled that, despite the fact that Marbury appeared to have a legal right to his commission, it was beyond the power of the Court to uphold that right.

The problem was that Marshall wanted to rule in favor of Marbury.[8] If he did so, he might publicly embarrass the new president and score a political victory for the Federalists. However, Marshall recognized that the Court had no means to enforce its decisions. If he ruled in favor of Marbury, Jefferson and Madison could—and probably would—simply ignore the Court. Jefferson had popular support, and a presidential refusal to support the Court would not only be a blow to the Federalists, but would also cripple the Court and make it obvious that the judiciary had very little power.

Chief Justice Marshall chose a politically astute compromise. He ruled that it was beyond the power of the Court to uphold Marbury's right to the commission. By ruling that Marbury had a right to the appointment, Marshall was able to scold and embarrass the president. And by ruling that the Court did not have the power to right the wrong done to Marbury, Marshall avoided a politically self-defeating decision.

Marshall solved his dilemma by ruling that Section 13 of the congressional Judiciary Act of 1789 was unconstitutional. By this act, Congress empowered the Supreme Court to "issue writs of mandamus in cases warranted by the principles and usages of law, to courts appointed, or persons holding office, under the authority of the United States." A writ of mandamus was the tool the Court needed to force Madison to serve Marbury's commission. But Marshall ruled that the Court could not uphold the law Congress enacted because, "the authority . . . given to the Supreme Court, by the Act . . . appears not to be warranted by the Constitution."[9]

Marshall was relying on the rarely used doctrine of judicial review. Legal scholar Henry J. Abraham has defined judicial review as:

> The power of any court to hold unconstitutional and hence unenforceable any law, any official action based upon a law and any other action by a public official that it deems upon careful, normally painstaking, reflection and in line with the taught traditions of the law as well as judicial self-restraint — to be in conflict with the basic law, in the United States, its Constitution.[10]

In essence, Marshall said the judiciary had the power to overrule an act of Congress. This was a great deal more power than the traditional judicial role of settling disputes by judging facts and interpreting applicable rules and statutes. But if Marshall was going to use judicial review, he had to find a way to show that the use of such power fell within the legitimate role of the Court.

Marshall turned to the Constitution to justify his use of power. He had little precedent to rely on. "Certainly," Marshall said, "all those who have framed written constitutions contemplate them as forming the fundamental and paramount law of the nation, and consequently the theory of every such government must be, that an act of the legislature repugnant to the constitution, is void."[11] Marshall's language could not be found in the Constitution. The Chief Justice relied on logic and rhetoric rather than settled law. The Constitution did say, however, that "this Constitution, and the Laws of the United States which shall be made in Pursuance thereof . . . shall be the supreme Law of the Land."[12] Marshall said this meant that no law may violate the Constitution since the Constitution is the supreme law of the land. And, because the Court interpreted Section 13 of the Judiciary Act of 1789 to be in violation of the Constitution, it was the Court's duty to refuse to sustain the act as law.

But was it the Court's duty? The Constitution outlined a separation of powers. Article I established the role of the legislature. Article II established the role of the executive. Article III established the Supreme Court, but the language was vague about the Court's powers and duties. The Constitution could be interpreted to mean that the legislature or the president would take final responsibility for the constitutionality of governmental acts. The Constitution was not

explicit. But Marshall said it was "emphatically the province and duty
of the judicial department to say what the law is."[13] In that some cases
would require the judiciary to read and interpret the Constitution,
logic demanded that judges could not be "forbidden to read or to
obey" that compact, and obedience to the Constitution might well
mean overruling a congressional act.[14] Otherwise, Marshall asked,
"Why does a judge swear to discharge his duties agreeably to the
constitution of the United States if that constitution forms no rule for
his government?"[15]

Marshall, no stranger to politics, understood the need to wield
the Court's power cautiously. He went to great lengths in his written
opinion to justify the use of judicial review, a doctrine he did not use
again.

Many legal scholars and judges have since cited *Marbury* as
authority for the use of judicial review. But *Marbury* provided another,
equally valuable lesson for the judiciary that has become an axiom of
decision making. Judicial decisions must be justified in a politically
acceptable manner. The task is complicated because the powers
granted to the Court are not always explicit. The Supreme Court, in
fact, must determine for itself the correct role for the judiciary. The
result is that the Court must be conservative in its use of judicial
power or risk the public perception that the judiciary has acted illegiti-
mately. A loss of public confidence, as Marshall understood, always
holds the potential for weakening the Court's power and authority.
Constitutional scholar Archibald Cox stated the problem this way:
"[The judiciary] possesses neither the purse nor the sword. Constitu-
tionalism as a constraint upon the government depends, in the first
instance, upon the habit of voluntary compliance and, in the last
resort, upon a people's realization that their freedom depends upon
observance of the rule of law. The realization must be strong enough
for the community to rise up and overwhelm, morally and politically,
any notable offender."[16]

MCCULLOCH v. MARYLAND. The political les-
sons of *Marbury* were reaffirmed in 1819 in *McCulloch v. Maryland.*[17] In
McCulloch, Marshall was required to interpret the meaning of the
Constitution to determine the scope of certain congressional powers.

Congress had chartered a bank in Baltimore, Maryland. When

the state of Maryland charged that the federal government had no constitutional right to establish a national bank, it fell upon the Supreme Court to settle the dispute. Nowhere did the Constitution specifically give Congress power to charter a bank. Chief Justice Marshall pointed, however, to Article I, Section 8, Clause 13, which states, "The Congress shall have the power . . . to make all laws which shall be necessary and proper for carrying into execution the foregoing Powers, and all other Powers vested in this Constitution in the Government of the United States, or any Department or Officer thereof."

Marshall interpreted Clause 13 to mean that Congress had the right to charter a national bank. The decision was politically charged because it meant that Congress had broad authority to utilize powers that were not specifically enumerated in the Constitution, and once again it made the Supreme Court the final arbiter of what the Constitution meant. Marshall recognized the gravity of the situation and stated in the first paragraph of his decision: "No tribunal can approach such a question without a deep sense of its importance, and of the awful responsibility involved in its decision. But it must be decided peacefully, or remain a source of hostile legislation, perhaps of hostility of still a more serious nature; and if it is to be so decided, by this tribunal alone can the decision be made. On the Supreme Court of the United States has the Constitution of our country devolved this important duty."[18]

Marshall recognized that he had to do more than settle the legal dispute. He also had to justify the Court's interpretation of the Constitution as a legitimate use of judicial power. Marshall explained that

> a constitution, to contain an accurate detail of all the subdivisions of which its great powers will admit, and of all the means by which they may be carried into execution, would partake of the prolixity of a legal code, and could scarcely be embraced by the human mind. It would probably never be understood by the public. Its nature, therefore, requires, that only its great outlines should be marked, its important objects be designated, and the minor ingredients which compose those objects be deduced from the nature of the objects themselves.[19]

It was the Court's duty to interpret the legal parameters for

Congress set by the Constitution. But any such interpretation was tempered by a respect for the separation of powers among the executive, legislative and judicial branches of government. The benefit of the doubt in *McCulloch* was given to Congress.

Marshall's opinion carefully justified the Court's use of power and explained where the Court's authority came from. The Constitution was not explicit. But Marshall's logic wove a fabric of judicial reasoning that could be perceived as well within the scope of the legitimate role of the judiciary. Marshall, as he had done in *Marbury*, accomplished three tasks in *McCulloch*. The Court settled the legal dispute before it. The Court made it clear that its role was to consider the dispute within its own interpretation of the Constitution. And the Court presented its decision in a way such that the use of judicial power would be perceived as legitimate.

OGDEN v. SAUNDERS. If *McCulloch* suggested the Court would give deference to legislatures when their actions were challenged on constitutional grounds, this case, decided in 1827, made it explicit that legislation would indeed come to the Court with a presumption of constitutionality.[20] The case required the Court to rule on a New York statute designed to aid debtors. The law was attacked as a violation of Article I, Section 10 of the Constitution, which forbids the government to impair the obligation of contracts. Writing for the majority, Justice Bushrod Washington said, "It is but a decent respect to the wisdom, integrity, and patriotism of the legislative body, by which any law is passed, to presume in favor of its validity, until its violation of the Constitution is proved beyond a reasonable doubt."[21] The Court upheld the constitutionality of the New York law.

Washington's decent respect for the wisdom of the legislature was more than polite respect. It was an acknowledgment of the separation of powers outlined in the Constitution. And it was an element of judicial decision making based on the understanding that the Court cannot breach certain parameters of judicial authority. The boundaries of judicial power were not defined explicitly in the Constitution or committed to paper in a single volume of rules. The rules were vital, nevertheless, to the maintenance of judicial legitimacy and, for that reason, these unwritten rules affected the decision-making process just as much as any statute that came before the Court.

BARRON V. BALTIMORE. It is clear from the above cases that the Supreme Court has the authority to interpret the Constitution. Such interpretations, however, are not based on judicial perceptions of what is morally right. While the Bill of Rights does establish certain rights for individual citizens, the Constitution also provides a binding structure for the governance of the nation as a whole. When the Court decides a case, it must consider both individual rights and governmental structure. *Barron v. Baltimore* is a case in point.[22]

Barron owned a warehouse alongside a Baltimore, Maryland, stream. When the city undertook some road construction, much of the stream was filled with sand and silt and the warehouse was rendered useless for offloading ships. Barron sued, claiming that the Fifth Amendment forbade local as well as federal government from taking private property "without just compensation." The Fifth Amendment states, in part, that no person shall be "deprived of life, liberty, or property without due process of law; nor shall private property be taken for public use, without just compensation."

Marshall ruled that Barron was not protected by the Fifth Amendment. The Bill of Rights, Marshall said, "contain[s] no expression indicating an intention to apply them to state governments."[23] The Court was not deciding whether Barron's claim was moral. The federal government, in fact, could not have treated the wharf owner in the manner he was treated by his local government. But Marshall pointed out that "had the framers of these amendments intended them to be limitations on the powers of the state governments, they would have . . . expressed that intention."[24]

At first reading, Marshall's opinion appears simply to settle a legal dispute by drawing support from the Constitution. But the decision was more complex. Marshall also explained the role of the federal government in local disputes. Under the doctrine of federalism, the only authority the federal government had over local governments was the authority provided for by the Constitution. Settling Barron's dispute was important. But it was only one element of the Court's role. Marshall's jurisprudence also required that consideration be given to the overall political scheme outlined by the framers. The Court was not free to do as it pleased. Disputes had to be settled within the framework of a constitution that both established the governmental structure of the nation and protected the rights of individuals. Ignoring either of those elements risked the public perception of an illegitimate use of power by the Court.

DRED SCOTT v. SANFORD. In 1857 Chief Justice Roger Taney took just such a risk. In *Dred Scott v. Sanford* the Court attempted to play a role in the slavery issue that left it susceptible to the charge that it had gone far beyond its legitimate judicial role.[25]

Dred Scott was a slave in Missouri. His owner, however, took Scott to Illinois, a free state, and then into upper Louisiana Territory where slavery was outlawed by the Missouri Compromise of 1820. When Scott later returned to Missouri, he sued in state court claiming that, once freed, he could not be returned to slavery simply because he entered a slave state. Scott lost his case in the Missouri courts and appealed to the United States Supreme Court.[26]

The political implications inherent in Scott's case were immense. The nation was already divided over slavery and Congress had failed to reach a satisfactory compromise solution. Even so, the Supreme Court could have settled Scott's case with a minimum of public controversy. Seven years earlier the Court ruled that legal disputes involving slavery were covered by state rather than federal law.[27] Because Scott was considered a slave under Missouri law, precedent existed for the Court to avoid a constitutional battle by giving deference to Missouri's legislature and courts. The practice of deferring to legislatures was already well established, and the Supreme Court had good reason to do so in Scott's case. Any other course carried the risk of having to address three controversial and political questions. Did a slave lose slave status permanently by traveling from a slave state into a free territory? Did Congress even have the constitutional authority to ban slavery from the territories? And did Scott hold the prerequisite of Missouri citizenship necessary to sue in the federal courts?

The Court did not exist in a vacuum in 1857, and problems that plagued the nation were mirrored on the bench. The justices felt they "had to say something, not just about one slave, but about all slaves," according to historian Bruce Catton.[28] Chief Justice Roger Taney quickly realized that any attempt at compromise to reach a unanimous opinion would be futile. Worse, Taney was under pressure from President James Buchanan to settle the slavery issue once and for all because it had become a political liability. Taney decided to plunge into the controversy and to write the opinion himself.

Ruling against Scott, Chief Justice Taney said the former slave was not a legal citizen of Missouri and had no right to sue in the federal courts. Furthermore, the Chief Justice applied the doctrine of judicial review to the Missouri Compromise and ruled that Congress had no constitutional authority to ban slavery from the territories. It was the Missouri Compromise that had made Scott a free man to begin with, but since that law was now declared invalid, it was moot to ask whether Scott was still free when he returned to a slave state.

The lesson from the Marshall Court was a lesson of jurisprudence. Supreme Court decisions must settle disputes, and disputes must be settled in a manner in keeping with the accepted role of the judiciary. But the Taney Court ignored or was unable to follow Marshall's example. Taney attempted to command too broad a role for the Court. The public was unwilling to allow nine unelected justices to settle such a burning question of national policy. Attacks on the Court came from every corner as the justices were accused of exceeding their legitimate authority. Abraham Lincoln loathed the decision and he railed at the Court's political policy making during his inaugural address.

> If the policy of the government, upon vital questions, affecting the whole people, is to be irrevocably fixed by decisions of the Supreme Court, the instant they are made, in ordinary litigation between parties, in personal actions, the people will have ceased to be their own rulers, having to that extent, practically resigned their government into the hands of that eminent tribunal.[29]

The Dred Scott decision made it clear that the Court cannot stand as a solitary oracle of what the nation's laws and values should be. The Court may interpret the Constitution. But the judiciary is only one element in a three-part system of government. If the Court attempts to take on the kind of policy-making role normally reserved for the legislature, it must be able to defend its extension of judicial power or else lose its major strength—the public's perception and acceptance of the Court's legitimacy. Legal scholar G. Edward White stated the problem succinctly. "The legitimacy of judicial decisions," White said, "rests on the public's willingness to accept the expertise and authority of the judicial office, which is itself based on the ability of judges to persuade by a process of reasoning in their opinions."[30]

Why did the Taney Court fail when the Marshall Court had succeeded? The Marshall Court did not have specific language in the Constitution to bolster its decisions in *Marbury* or *McCulloch*. Yet Marshall was able to cull from the Constitution certain principles the nation shared and believed in. Taney's jurisprudence in *Dred Scott* did not take those principles into account. Without the foundation of public belief that the Court is acting within its legitimate role, according to White, "the judiciary can no longer effectively function, for its legitimacy rests on its separation from and transcendence of partisan discourse. If a court may be judged to have entered the political arena and is criticized on that arena's terms, as the Taney Court was after *Dred Scott*, it cannot help but lose stature."[31] The Taney Court's jurisprudence had failed.

Axioms of Judicial Decision Making

The Supreme Court maintains its legitimate role among the legislative and executive branches of government by acting, or refusing to act, in a particular manner in any given case. At least one element of the judicial role is to function as a check on abuses by the other branches of government in what is termed the checks and balances system. The judicial review doctrine practiced in *Marbury v. Madison* is an example of the power to act as a check on the legislature. Yet the Court cannot overuse its power, as it did in *Dred Scott*, without upsetting the balance among the elements of government. In response to the need for a stable balance the Court usually operates within the restrictions of another axiom. Henry Abraham stated the Court's code of behavior this way: "The Supreme Court . . . is not designed to serve as a check against inept, unwise, emotional, unrepresentative legislators."[32]

In practice, this axiom is seen as deference to the legislature. The Court may eventually find a law unconstitutional, but it is not the Court's role to overturn an otherwise constitutional statute simply because the justices see the act as undesirable. The distinction between undesirable and unconstitutional law can be a fine one, yet ignoring the distinction would place the Court into the role of superlegislature and raise the question of whether the judiciary operated outside of its legitimate role.[33] Chief Justice Morrison Waite stated the point clearly in the Court's response to an 1877 challenge to the constitutionality of an Illinois law regulating grain elevator rates. "We know that this is a power," Waite wrote for the majority, "which may be abused; but that is no argument against its existence. For protection against abuses by legislatures the people must resort to the polls."[34]

The Court's role is a complex element of American government. Because the Constitution is vague about the judicial role, it falls upon the judiciary to establish and define the parameters of its own judicial powers. The primary safeguard against judicial abuse is the Court's understanding that it must be perceived as acting within the boundaries of its legitimate institutional role.

The Supreme Court role contains a number of elements, and each element exerts a force on the others. The most basic duty of the Court is to settle legal disputes. Who is legally correct, party A or party B? To make that decision the Court interprets the law by attempting to determine what the framers of the Constitution meant, what Congress meant when it passed an act or statute, how the courts decided past cases. Each of these elements of decision making, however, is tempered by judicial axioms of conduct. The axioms can be summarized as follows:[35]

> a) The Court must justify its decisions and demonstrate that they are based on a legitimate use of judicial authority.

> b) Judicial interpretations of the law must bear in mind the constitutionally mandated separation of powers.

> c) Legislation carries a presumption of constitutionality.

d) The Court's task is to decide what the law is rather than whether a specific claim appears moral or just.

e) Social policy making is a job for the legislature, not the judiciary.

f) The remedy for undesirable legislation is available through the electoral process rather than through the courts.

The amount of discretion the Court has when it interprets the law is affected by the above axioms, which are derived from the Court's interpretation of its role within the constitutional scheme of government. Judicial opinions must show explicitly that the Court is using a legitimate power, or must be based on a judicial use of power that is already well accepted. Professor Shapiro stated the problem succinctly:

> Several commentators have pointed out that the Court's duty to square its decisions with reason and authority is the key to its accountability and responsibility to the public . . . But the Justices' work might just as well be viewed as a continuous attempt to convince the public that the Court's decisions are constitutionally legitimate. The necessity of justifying every decision publicly is a restraint placed on few other government officials. If it is naive to believe that the Court can be wholly limited by a self-interpreted Constitution, it is certainly equally naive to believe that the Justices are totally unrestrained by provisions to which they must continually and publicly pay homage. Indeed, it is the most modest among the judges who constantly prove that the courts sincerely feel bound by constitutional obligations. The greatest restraint on the Court is, of course, the judicial process itself.[36]

How far can the Court go in overruling legislation before it will be perceived as going beyond its legitimate authority? Justice Marshall found the necessary support in *Marbury* to overrule an act of Congress. Taney's *Dred Scott* decision was unenforceable. There is no one rule or set of guidelines for the Court to follow. But the traditions and history of the Court do provide Supreme Court justices with an outline of what is acceptable. Together, the Constitution and the axioms of judicial decision making that have been handed down since the Court's inception give the Court the potential to operate in a manner that can be defended from the attacks of its critics.

Each Supreme Court justice has his or her own jurisprudence — his or her own philosophy that governs the outcome of decisions. From the Court's earliest days justices have learned that their jurisprudence must take into account the law and the role of the judiciary. Their perceptions of the judicial role have, in turn, affected their application of the law.

Justice Oliver Wendell Holmes was only a child when Roger Taney wrote the opinion in *Dred Scott,* and his familiarity with John Marshall came only from reading. Nevertheless, Holmes was no stranger to the judicial axioms that preceded him. Late in his career, Holmes told sixty-one-year-old Justice Harlan Fiske Stone, "Young man, about seventy-five years ago I learned that I was not God. And so, when the people . . . want to do something I can't find anything in the Constitution expressly forbidding them to do, I say, whether I like it or not, 'Godamnit, let 'em do it.' "[37] Holmes, in a colorful manner, was expressing his belief in the supremacy of the Constitution and in the power of the electorate. Both factors were major elements of Holmes's personal jurisprudence.

6

Holmes and the Judicial Role

Certainly however disdainfully Holmes repudiated pragmatism as a philosophy of life, he accepted it as a philosophy of law. He was the first, and remained the greatest, of legal pragmatists. Basic to his philosophy of law was the principle that law is no finished thing, no absolute, but still in the making; that it derives neither from God nor from Nature, less from history than most scholars believed and less from logical analysis than jurists supposed, but largely from experience.

HENRY STEELE COMMAGER, 1950,
The American Mind

OLIVER WENDELL HOLMES, JR., has fascinated the American public as well as the legal community. No other Supreme Court justice could open the arts section of the newspaper to find himself the central focus of a Broadway play and few have been the object of as much analysis.[1] Holmes was appointed to the Court at age sixty-one and, when Holmes had served eighteen years as an associate justice, Harvard law professor Roscoe Pound wrote that "above all others [Holmes] has shaped the methods and ideas that are characteristic of the present as distinguished from the immediate past."[2] Holmes remained a driving force on the Court for another decade.

Not everyone praised Holmes as Pound did. H. L. Mencken reviewed a collection of Holmes's dissenting opinions in 1930 and wrote, "If this is liberalism, then all I can say is liberalism is not what it was when I was young."[3] At the end of World War II, an uncomplimentary article, "Hobbs, Holmes and Hitler," appeared in the prestigious *American Bar Association Journal*.[4] The thesis of the article was that Holmes's view of the judicial role was dangerous because it led him to uphold a law whether or not he thought the law was a wise one.

Labels such as liberal and conservative are sometimes assigned to Supreme Court justices by critics and scholars. Holmes would have challenged their usefulness, although as a private citizen he held strong views. He was concerned with philosophy and literature, a boyhood friend of William James, and graduated from Harvard College in 1861 as class poet, the same honor his father had received in 1832. Holmes was a lifelong Republican. He was wounded severely three times in the Civil War fighting for the Union cause. But the law to Holmes was something separate from politics and causes. Law was not to be understood as politically liberal or conservative, but as a systematic approach that aimed for sciencelike consistency. Legal scholar G. Edward White wrote that "Holmes's *The Common Law*, his contemporaries felt, was in the mainstream of the scientific movement in that it systematized jurisprudence on the basis of observable social phenomena rather than through intellectual abstractions."[5]

Holmes grew up in a Boston Brahmin family with close ties to intellectuals and literary masters such as James, Longfellow, and Emerson. His father was a doctor and a published author. And Holmes took his law degree from Harvard when the Civil War ended. Each of these biographical elements might be combined to suggest an explanation for Holmes's legal reasoning. Surely they might help to understand Holmes as an individual. But they are unnecessary to describe either how Holmes decided specific legal issues or to analyze his legal philosophy. A description of Holmes's judicial decision making can be constructed from his own writing. His legal opinions and dissents provide the basis of Chapter 7. This chapter focuses on an example of Holmes's writing off the bench in order to identify and analyze his legal philosophy.

The Path of the Law

Oliver Wendell Holmes came to Boston University School of Law on January 8, 1887, to deliver an address at the dedication of a new hall. He was well known in the legal community. He had been a member of the Massachusetts Bar for thirty years. His practice began with the prestigious Boston firm Chandler, Shattuck and Thayer, and he later developed his own partnership with Shattuck. He had already been a full professor at Harvard Law School and had been serving as an associate justice of the Massachusetts Supreme Court for five years. His publication, in 1881, of *The Common Law* brought critical acclaim in Europe as well as in the United States. His audience on this day was a gathering of law students and his address was entitled "The Path of the Law."

Holmes first sentence was deceptively simple. "When we study the law," Holmes said, "we are not studying a mystery but a well known profession."[6] What followed was more complex and raised two major issues. What *is* the law, and what *should* the law be? They were not esoteric questions.

American law changed in the late nineteenth century. Christopher Columbus Langdell became the first dean of the Harvard Law School in 1870 and used his appointment to alter radically legal education. Langdell believed that law should be treated as a science. The case law approach is today familiar to all law students, but Langdell's new method was severely attacked for a generation after he introduced it to Harvard.

There were other changes, not the least of which were caused by technology and industrialization. During the 1880s West Publishing Company brought out the National Reporter System. For the first time, lawyers throughout the nation had relatively easy access to state and federal appellate decisions.

The attitudes of judges also were changing. Before the Civil War many judges, faced with new situations and a dearth of consistent precedent, "created the law" in their courtrooms. But after the war, according to legal scholar Grant Gilmore, the judiciary viewed its role differently. "The judicial function [had] nothing to do with the adaptation of rules of law to changing conditions," Gilmore said. "It [was] restricted to the discovery of what the true rules of law are and indeed always [had] been."[7] In other words, the judiciary operated as if a legal rule already existed for whatever case might arise. The judge only needed to determine the proper legal rule to apply to the case at hand.

"The Path of the Law" announced Holmes's view of law as a

duality, and his address was looked upon as the beginning of a change by the legal profession in attitudes about the law. He began by defining what the law is, and then contrasted that definition with an element that exerts a constant tension on the practice of law; that is, a conception of what the law should be. Holmes's construction of these two distinct elements of law helps to explain the legal reasoning he used twenty-two years later in the *Schenck* decision as well as the path of logic that led critics such as Mencken to question the justice's liberalism.

Law, Holmes told the students, is the will of a majority of the people formalized as legislation. Law was not a question of morality or ethics, but a system of codified behavior. The function of law was to establish rules. The rules were not meant to tell the members of a society how to live, but to tell them what they must expect if the rules were broken. For this function to meet with success, the law had to be predictable.

"The first thing for a businesslike understanding of the matter," Holmes said, "is to understand its limits, and therefore I think it desirable at once to point out and dispel a confusion between morality and law."[8] In other words, whether law was good or bad in a moral sense made no difference. A law was something to be obeyed. Law could not "consider the right or the duty as something existing apart from and independent of the consequences of its breach."[9] If the law was breached, morality was not a question for the courts. Predictability was, and so the law required some response in the guise "of the public force through the instrumentality of the courts."[10]

Immediately a definitional problem arises that identifies Holmes's duality. Is judicial law the same thing as legislative law? There are two answers. Both yes and no are correct.

Holmes saw judicial and legislative law as the same in the sense that courts decide cases based on laws passed by the legislature. "In societies like ours," Holmes said, "the command of the public force is entrusted to judges in certain cases, and the whole power of the state will be put forth, if necessary, to carry out their judgments and decrees."[11] In other words, the codified rules of the legislature, assuming, of course, they do not violate the Constitution, are the laws the courts must use. And, for both the legislature and the judiciary, the law must be consistent. Consistency within the codification of rules gives legislative law the potential of predictability. "People want to know," Holmes told his audience, "under what circumstances and how far they will run the risk of coming against what is so much stronger than themselves."[12] The courts uphold their end of ensuring predictability by interpreting and applying the law consistently. The "power of the state" entrusted to judges is not the power to create law; it is a power to apply the law already set forth by the legislature.

The law, then, is a system for predictions, and the consistency of those predictions was, to Holmes, the essence of the judicial role. "The primary rights and duties with which jurisprudence busies itself," Holmes said, "again are nothing but prophecies."[13]

But judicial law differs from legislative law in an important way that manifests itself in the judicial role.[14] Judges are far less free than legislators to determine what the law *should* be. Judges may only enforce the law that *is*. A legislator is free to revise a statute, to decide that a new rule should take the place of an old one, and even to make a complete about-face as to what the law should be. All that is necessary is a vote, and, once the vote is taken, the legislature has determined what the law *is*. The judiciary has no such flexibility, and it is extremely rare for a court to reverse itself completely in its application of the law. The difference, then, is that the courts may not determine what the law *should* be in the same sense as the legislature. Judges may only enforce the law that *is*. When a legislature deals with law, it is law that may be created, amended or discarded. Judicial interpretations of the law may vary, but they are supposed to be rooted in the axiom that the intent of a legal rule is established by the legislature rather than the court.

Holmes did not see the law in a vacuum. He recognized the danger of divorcing morality from judicial law. "It is certain," Holmes said, "that many laws have been enforced in the past, and it is likely that some are enforced now, which are condemned by the most enlightened opinion of the time, or which at all events pass the limits of interference as many consciences would draw it."[15] Holmes returned, however, to what he viewed as the greater danger of allowing moral philosophies into judicial law.

"Nothing but confusion of thought," Holmes said, "can result from assuming that the rights of a man in a moral sense are equally rights in the sense of the Constitution and the law."[16] Bringing moral arguments into a judicial context, Holmes believed, would cause the entire proceeding "to drop into fallacy."[17] The result would be judicial fiats rather than predictable law. Holmes saw no more use for morals in a judicial argument than for a lawyer to describe the clothes a client was wearing when a contract was drawn up. The law is applied the same, Holmes pointed out, no matter what color hat the client is wearing. And so with judicial law and morality, the judge may deal with "only the facts of legal import, up to the final analysis and abstract universals of theoretic jurisprudence."[18] A judge's personal view of morality could play no part in a legal dispute.

This is not to suggest that Holmes was an immoral or an amoral man. Little could be further from the truth. But he felt, perhaps with the exception of cases decided on equity law, that the realm of the courts could not legitimately cross the line into the area of legislative law. Any attempt to do so would mean an end to predictability and, if judicial law was not predictable, then it served little use in a democracy.

Holmes was attempting to instruct law students and he understood that the legal philosophy he constructed was not an accurate description of daily judicial activities.

What transpired daily in American courtrooms? Holmes saw forces that determined the law's "content and its growth."[19] At the heart of these elements was the fallacy that "the only force at work in the development of the law is logic."[20] Logic had its place. Judges determined what they felt to be the proper rule in any given case through the use of logic and deduction. But the danger, Holmes told his audience, was "the notion that a given system, ours, for instance, can be worked out like mathematics from some general axioms of conduct."[21] Such a belief overlooked the familiar phenomenon of two judges reaching opposing conclusions based on an identical set of facts. This was based on the fallacy, Holmes said, that "one side or the other were not doing their sums right, and if they would take more trouble, agreement inevitably would come."[22] That might be true if there were a single correct interpretation of law. But this was not the case. There was room for honest disagreement.

If pure logic in the law was illusory, Holmes believed that "behind the logical form lies a judgment as to the relative worth and importance of competing legislative grounds, often an inarticulate and unconscious judgment, it is true, and yet the very root and nerve of the whole proceeding."[23]

Holmes was skeptical about the practice of law in the courts, but he was not a cynic. "I take it that no hearer of mine," he told the law students, "will misinterpret what I have to say as the language of cynicism."[24]

Certainly judicial law should treat the law for what it is rather than for what it should be. That was necessary for predictability. But the problem was that the methodology of judicial decision making was not always capable of leading to an exact logical conclusion.

Holmes was dealing with a timeworn legal issue, but he was adding new depth and insight to the problem. Law at the end of the nineteenth century, like many other disciplines, came under the spell of science and the belief that scientific methodology could provide a clear path through a forest of heretofore unsolvable problems. Holmes approved of the consistency and predictability inherent in scientific method. Surely this was better than a system of "natural" law that enabled judges to base their decisions on unpredictable notions of basic human rights. But even using science and deduction, Holmes warned, "you can give any conclusion a logical form."[25]

A good deal of the problem lay in the fact that at any moment in history, the legislative law that reflected the value and will of the majority was subject to change. Competing ideas were not absolute answers that were morally right or wrong. They were only different answers based on changing social norms. And as for logic as a tool to find the "right" answer, Holmes told his audience that "if anyone thinks that it can be settled deductively, or once and for all, I can only say that I think he is theoretically wrong, and that I am certain that his conclusion will not be accepted in practice *semper ubique et ab omnibus* [always, everywhere and by everyone]."[26]

For Holmes, these tensions did not present a dilemma. They served only to reinforce his notion that courts must strive for predictability and that the means to that end was not through individualistic judicial notions of basic rights. Judges first had to be aware that laws were relative and subject to change by the legislature and interpretation by the courts. Nevertheless, judges had to do their best to uphold the law as it stood, aware of competing forces, but attempting to rise above them. Logic and deduction could be used by the courts. But it should not be and was not within the realm of the courts to go the next step — to use logic and deduction as a rationale for substituting a judge's personal views for legislative law.

The system was imperfect, but to Holmes the alternative to

consistency and predictability was anarchy. Holmes preferred the duty to enforce a bad or inequitable law over a judicial ability to substitute a personal sense of basic moral rights. Holmes's task was the long-term goal: predictable and rational law. But what was rational?

The answer was troubling to American courts at the close of the nineteenth century. The introduction of Fourteenth Amendment arguments based on due process of law encouraged the courts to turn from their reliance on statutes and common law to constitutional interpretations that appeared to create new rights.[27] Some judges saw the Fourteenth Amendment as allowing them to rule on the constitutionality of a variety of state laws that went beyond the context of the concerns under which the amendment was drafted; that is, discrimination against newly freed southern blacks. Obviously, this view created a need among judges to do more than interpret the meaning of a state statute. Some judges also were deciding whether legislatures had acted properly to begin with in enacting certain statutes. Supreme Court scholar Richard Cortner stated that "many . . . saw the Due Process Clause as the vehicle by which the Court was imposing some of its most reactionary decisions on the states. The vagueness of the Due Process Clause, it was felt, allowed the justices to roam at large and to read into it their personal political, social and economic views as part of the Constitution."[28]

Holmes opposed what today would be called "activist" tampering with the Constitution. It was, to Holmes, a violation of the judicial role to find new rights in the Constitution. The judge's duty was to be limited to upholding the law as it stood. Professor Walter Goedecke wrote that Holmes "opposed the classic thought of rights and duties and judicial limits on governmental powers on every ground and in every way. Justice Holmes did not believe in rights. Again and again he said they were a false beginning for the law, which instead should be understood in terms of irrational and factional beginnings in history and nonrational and largely unwise goals deemed expedient by most people at whatever times these feelings are active."[29]

Holmes feared activist interpretations of due process had "led people who no longer hope to control the legislature to look to the courts as expounders of the Constitution."[30] He pointed out that in some courts "new principles have been discovered outside the bodies of those instruments."[31] Finally, Holmes said that such approaches left much to be desired. "I cannot but believe that if the training of lawyers led them habitually to consider more definitely and explicitly the social advantage on which the rule they lay down must be justified, they sometimes would hesitate where now they are confident, and see that really they were taking sides upon debatable and often burning questions."[32] Such questions were not for judicial law. They were the province of legislative law.

Whose responsibility was it then to deal with what the law should be? Holmes addressed just that question in the second half of his lecture. He told the students that the study of law should be rational. Attorneys should address not only what the law is, but what it should be. Here Holmes questioned the overall rationality of following the rule simply because the rule existed. Yes, that rule had to be followed by the courts as long as it was the legislative law, but legislative law was subject to change. "It is revolting to have no better reason for a rule of law than that it was so laid down in the time of Henry IV," Holmes said.[33]

Holmes believed social science was a tool to identify what the public wanted a particular law to accomplish and then to discern the best type of law to accomplish that goal. "What have we better than a blind guess," Holmes asked, "to show that the criminal law in its present form does more good than harm?"[34] Holmes questioned the impact on society of jailing lawbreakers and wondered out loud whether punishment actually deterred crime.

To Holmes, knowing the form of the law was not sufficient. Lawyers should be concerned "with the ends sought to be attained and the reasons for desiring them."[35] But such study should not be confused with the duty of the judge. Holmes the liberal, the scholar, the philosopher, was well aware of the limits of the law as it was announced by the legislature. He foresaw a more rational method of legislating the rules of a society. But he also was aware of the limits that must be placed on the judicial role in order to maintain a legal system founded on predictability. Holmes's lesson for the Boston University law class was that two kinds of law exist: judicial law and legislative law. The law students were advised to be concerned with both and to be aware of the limits of each. Anything less promised confusion in the courtroom and inevitable conflict over the legitimate role of the courts. The ultimate goal was perhaps beyond attainment, but striving for that goal was the job of the courts.

7

Holmes's Judicial Decision Making

Two things about Justice Oliver Wendell Holmes need reconciliation. He had a very bad philosophy. Yet he ranks among the greatest men of our time. His philosophy was agnostic, materialistic, hopeless of the attainment of any ultimate truth, meaning or standard of value. As a result, it is fundamentally indistinguishable from the amoral realism of those regimes of force and power that are the scandal of the century.

HAROLD MCKINNON, 1950

66"The Path of the Law" stressed the importance of predictability in law.[1] The law was not a set of rules designed to tell the "good" man how to live. Law to Oliver Wendell Holmes was a codified system reflecting the will of the majority from which a person could determine what action society, through the courts, would take if the code was violated. Assuming Holmes attempted to practice on the bench the legal philosophy he constructed in "The Path of the Law," it should be possible to identify the consistent presence of certain elements in his judicial decision making. Those elements, for Holmes at least, would be necessary to make the law predictable.

Two tenets of judicial philosophy can be identified in "The Path of the Law" lecture. Holmes believed both were necessary to ensure predictability. The first can be stated as: Judicial law must treat the law as it *is*, rather than as a judge might think that it *should* be. From this doctrine a question can be formulated and applied to specific judicial writings by Holmes to determine whether in practice he treated the law as it *was* rather than as he *might wish it to be*. Did Holmes decide cases based on specific, enumerated principles of law rather than on a personal notion of what the rational response of society should be? References to legal doctrines such as "inherent rights" found by the courts would suggest the latter. Reliance on specific statutes and settled principles of common law would be good indicators of the former.

Holmes's second legal tenet can be stated as: Law is the will of the majority, rational or not, as reflected in the legislature and codified in the form of written statutes and acts. Holmes understood, of course, that legislation is always subordinate to the Constitution and that the Court has the duty to declare invalid any law that violates the national charter. The judicial review doctrine was firmly established in *Marbury v. Madison* almost one hundred years before "The Path of the Law" address.[2] Nevertheless, Holmes believed that, whenever possible, the Court should interpret legislation in a manner that would keep it within the parameters of what is constitutionally permissible. In essence, the Constitution created a democracy capable of governmental experimentation within certain limits. Only when a law explicitly violated the Constitution did the Court have the authority to eschew the majority will and force legislation back within those constitutional limits.[3]

Two questions are useful in identifying whether Holmes's belief in the will of the majority played a role in his judicial decision making. First, did Holmes apply a presumption of constitutionality to legislation challenged before the Court as unconstitutional? Under a presumption of constitutionality, the Court begins its deliberations with the assumption that the legislation before it is constitutional. The burden of proof to show otherwise rests upon the party challenging the legislation in question. In 1938, however, Justice Harlan Fiske Stone hinted in dicta in *United States v. Carolene Products* that the Court would apply stricter standards to laws challenged as infringements upon individual rights found in the first ten amendments to the Constitution. "There may be narrower scope," Stone wrote in footnote 4, "for operation of the presumption of constitutionality when legislation appears on its face to be within a specific prohibition of the Constitution, such as those of the first ten amendments, which are deemed equally specific when held to be embraced within the Fourteenth."[4]

Deference to the legislative will would be an indication that Holmes was not prone to using the Constitution to justify the substitution of his personal beliefs for those of the legislative majority.

And second, did Holmes apply a narrow construction to the meaning of any given statute or act before the courts? A positive answer here would indicate that, again, Holmes did not want to inflict his own notion of rational legislative behavior over what he perceived to be the will of the majority.

If the answers to these questions are consistently positive, then it is possible to assume that some basic components of Holmes's decision making have been identified. This also would suggest an ability to predict and explain with some validity Holmes's judicial reasoning. In the language of the legal community, we will have identified Holmes's jurisprudence.

The nine judicial opinions below are examples of Holmes's work prior to *Schenck v. United States.*[5] Some were dissenting opinions. Some involved freedom of expression. Each involved legal issues that prompted Holmes to explain why he constructed his judicial decisions in a particular manner. Holmes wrote more than one thousand opinions on the Massachusetts Supreme Court before serving a twenty-nine-year term on the United States Supreme Court.[6] The cases selected cover a fourteen-year time span from 1893 to 1917. While it is not possible to comment here on all of Holmes's judicial writing, the selection below is representative of the justice's judicial decision making between "The Path of the Law" address at Boston College and his 1919 opinion in *Schenck.*

HANSON v. GLOBE. This 1893 libel case provided the occasion for Holmes, an associate justice on the Massachusetts Supreme Court, to remind his brethren of the importance of predictability in law.[7] The *Boston Globe* had reported the arrest and drunkenness of a south Boston real estate broker the paper identified as H. P. Hanson. Unfortunately for the *Globe,* H. P. Hanson sued. The man actually arrested was A. H. P. Hanson.

The court majority decided the case turned on a question of whether the newspaper intentionally libeled the plaintiff. If there was no intention to harm H. P. Hanson, there was an absence of malice and without such malice, the court said, the newspaper was not culpable for its mistake. The court ruled there was an absence of malice.

Justice Holmes dissented. He believed the majority had applied an extralegal interpretation of malice and libel rather than following previously established principles of law. Holmes said precedent clearly precluded the justices from considering whether the *Globe* actually intended to harm the plaintiff. The only question, Holmes said, was whether the newspaper in fact defamed H. P. Hanson.

"In view of the unfortunate use of the word 'malice' in connection with libel and slander," Holmes scolded, "a doubt may be felt whether the actions for these causes are governed by general principles."[8] To Holmes, the specific facts of the case were important only so far as they determined which rule of law to apply. The question of intended harm or malice had no bearing on that decision. The definition of malice the court used was no longer law, Holmes said. "For a long time it has been held that the malice alleged in an action of libel means no more than it does in any other actions of torts."[9]

Holmes treated *Hanson v. Globe* as a case requiring the application of a narrow rule of law. It was outside the judicial role to reinterpret the meaning of libel if precedent already provided a definition. It should also be noted that no mention was made of First Amendment issues, despite what we might see today as inherent free speech implications. Two years later Holmes was explicit about his reasons for avoiding constitutional issues in another case involving speech and again showed his penchant for a narrow interpretation of the law.

COMMONWEALTH v. DAVIS. William F. Davis was charged with violating a local ordinance when he preached the gospel on the Boston Commons. The ordinance made it a crime to give a public address, offer goods for sale, or shoot off a cannon on the Commons without a permit from the mayor. Williams had no such permit.

Holmes wrote the opinion in the 1895 case of the *Commonwealth v. Davis* for the Massachusetts Supreme Court.[10] He immediately stated that the only question before the court was the meaning of the ordinance Williams allegedly violated. Holmes dismissed any constitutional implications. "For the legislature absolutely or conditionally to forbid public speaking in a highway or public park," Holmes explained, "is no more an infringement on the rights of a member of the public than for the owner of a private house to forbid it in his house."[11]

Holmes's opinion demonstrated his belief that the Court should assume that legislative bodies act with good intentions. Unless the defendant can prove otherwise, any given statute will be considered constitutional. "It is argued that the ordinance really is directed especially against the free preaching of the gospel in public places, as certain Western ordinances seemingly general have been held to be directed against the Chinese. But we have no reason to believe, and do not believe, that this ordinance was passed for any other than its ostensible purpose, namely, as a proper regulation of the use of public grounds."[12] There was a presumption of constitutionality on Holmes's part that precluded searching for more basic rights in the Constitution. Deference had to be given to the majority voice that appeared as legislation.

Finally, Holmes reiterated that all that was necessary was to find the meaning of the statute involved. "It follows that, as we have said at the outset, the only question open is the construction of the ordinance. We are of the opinion that the words 'No person shall . . . make any public address,' in the Revised Ordinances . . . have as broad a meaning as the words 'No person shall deliver a sermon.' "[13] In other words, the only need for logic and deduction on the court's part was to interpret the will of the legislature. Were sermons the same as public addresses? All other considerations were outside the authority of the court. A specific principle of law was followed—in this case, the local ordinance. The social ramifications of the ordinance, even its rationality, were beyond the scope of the court.

On December 1, 1902, President Theodore Roosevelt nominated Oliver Wendell Holmes, Jr., for a seat on the United States Supreme Court. The nomination was confirmed two days later by a voice vote in the Senate. Roosevelt's Justice Department was intent at that time on breaking up big business trusts. Within a year and a half, however, Holmes's jurisprudence brought the justice into conflict with some of Roosevelt's trust-busting plans.

NORTHERN SECURITIES COMPANY v. UNITED STATES. This was a complex case decided by the United

States Supreme Court in 1903, in which disagreement over judicial approaches split the justices into a 5–4 decision.[14] The case pivoted upon the Court's interpretation of the federal Sherman Antitrust Act. Northern Securities was accused of violating the act because its acquisitions appeared to be aimed at eliminating competition among certain railroads. Holmes could not agree with the Court's finding that the act was violated and wrote a dissent that brought into focus much of his philosophy about judicial decision making.

Holmes began with one of his most frequently quoted statements: "Great cases like hard cases make bad law. For great cases are called great, not by reason of their real importance in shaping the law of the future, but because of some accident of immediate overwhelming interest which appeals to the feelings and distorts the judgment. These immediate interests exercise a kind of hydraulic pressure which makes what previously was clear seem doubtful, and before which even well settled principles of law will bend."[15]

Holmes, again, was pointing out the need for consistency in the law. He recognized and warned that social and political pressures could sway the courts and lead the judiciary to substitute extralegal notions of law for long-standing and settled principles. Holmes felt that had happened to the majority in the present case. But Holmes also believed it possible to avoid such traps. The Court simply had to "find the meaning of some not very difficult words."[16] The words Holmes referred to were those of the antitrust act. Under Holmes's methodology the result would be the same for a controversial case as it would be for one "which excited no public attention, and was of importance only to a prisoner before the court."[17]

Holmes consistently turned to statutory interpretations to decide cases. This does not mean that he was unaware of, or that he refused to consider, constitutional implications in his judicial decision making. Holmes believed, however, that he must first make every attempt to settle cases without raising constitutional issues. And toward that end, as he pointed out in his dissent, "the statute must be construed in such a way as not merely to save its constitutionality but, so far as is consistent with a fair interpretation, not to raise grave doubts on that score."[18]

Two principles appear to lie behind this methodology. First, Holmes's deference to the legislature exemplified his belief that law was the will of the majority present in all legislation. In that legislation

was the most accurate pulse of the majority will, constitutional implications were to be acted on by the judiciary only when no other
avenue was available. Holmes believed the Court's job was to ad-
minister the law as it was written. If the Court could find a way to
read a statute as constitutional, then it was required to do so by the
scheme of governmental separation of powers outlined in the Constitution. Even if the Court's duties were not explicit in the Constitution,
the role of the judiciary in such situations, to Holmes, was implicit
and clear. The courts were not charged with second-guessing the
rationality of the public.

The second principle underlying Holmes's methodology in
Northern Securities was his desire to avoid substituting his own opinions
for settled precedent. The narrow interpretation of statutes and acts
enabled Holmes to justify, to himself and to the Court, his opinions as
logical and proper conclusions based only on the law as it was.

LOCHNER v. NEW YORK. This 1905 case again
placed Holmes on the dissenting side of a 5–4 decision.[19] *Lochner* is a
clear example of Holmes's belief in the will of the legislative majority
as a first principle of law.

The argument revolved around a New York law making it illegal
for bakery employees to work more than ten hours a day or a total of
sixty hours a week. The Court majority said the law was unconstitutional. The Court found that the statute violated the Fourteenth
Amendment right of due process in that it interfered with the individual right of contract.

The Court's reasoning emanated from *Allgeyer v. Louisiana,* decided in 1897.[20] In *Allgeyer* the Court reasoned the due process clause
in the Fourteenth Amendment was intended to protect the individual's right to "live and work where he will; to earn his livelihood by
any lawful calling; to pursue any livelihood or avocation, and for that
purpose to enter into all contracts which may be proper, necessary
and essential to his carrying out to a successful conclusion the purposes above mentioned."[21] If a bakery worker wanted to contract to
work more than ten hours a day, the legislature could not stop him.

Holmes found the Court's reasoning unacceptable and suggested
that the majority based its decision on a belief in laissez faire econom-
ics rather than on general principles of law. "This case is decided upon

an economic theory," Holmes said. But such theories, he continued, had "nothing to do with the right of a majority to embody their opinions in law."[22] This time the question before the Court was not how to interpret a statute, but whether the statute was even constitutional. To Holmes, economic preferences should have no part in a constitutional interpretation. "A constitution is not intended to embody a particular economic theory," Holmes said, "whether of paternalism and the organic relation of the citizen to the State or of *Laissez Faire*. It is made for people of fundamentally differing views."[23] Holmes's dissent can best be explained by turning to his reliance on the will of the majority. Holmes pointed out that it was "settled by various decisions of this court that state constitutions and state laws may regulate life in many ways which we as legislators might think as injudicious or if you like as tyrannical as this, and which equally with this interfere with the liberty to contract."[24] But evaluating the legislature's wisdom was not the Court's job. The Constitution was not a tool for overturning legislation the judiciary found ill-conceived. And Holmes found nothing in the Constitution prohibiting regulations such as the one in question. "The word liberty in the Fourteenth Amendment is perverted," Holmes said, "when it is held to prevent the natural outcome of a dominant opinion."[25] The Court strayed when it turned to constitutional interpretations that ignored settled principles. This made the law inconsistent and, therefore, unpredictable.

Some have pointed to *Lochner* as evidence that Holmes was a liberal on the Court. He appeared, in fact, to rule against big business in favor of labor and socially progressive legislation. The critics may be correct in their appreciation of the results of Holmes's dissent. They are wrong to suggest liberal politics had anything to do with that dissent. Holmes understood that specific cases were not always decided as they should be; that is, based on general principles of law. But he stated that his method of decision making was intended "to carry us far toward that end."[26] Consistency and deference to the legislative majority were the principles behind Holmes's judicial methodology. The liberal social outcome was never considered.

PATTERSON v. COLORADO. Three cases between 1907 and 1910 illustrate clearly that Holmes's decisions were based on a consistent judicial methodology rather than social progressivism. All three involved individual rights. *Patterson v. Colorado* (1907) involved, at least indirectly, freedom of expression.[27]

A Colorado newspaper editor was held in contempt of court after publishing articles and cartoons critical of the state supreme court. A number of legal issues were raised under appeal, but Holmes announced for an 8–1 majority that "the only question before this court is the power of the State."[28]

The specific facts of the situation weighed little on Holmes. "What constitutes contempt," Holmes said, "as well as the time during which it may be committed, is a matter of local law."[29] Once again, Holmes found that local law, not fundamental rights found in the United States Constitution, was the controlling principle of the case at hand. First Amendment implications were dismissed as irrelevant to the legal question before the Court. A remark by Holmes, however, must be noted. Justice Holmes pointed out that any question of whether the Fourteenth Amendment prohibited states from abridging speech in the same manner the First Amendment restricted the federal government would be left undecided.[30] Holmes was opposed to searching for general constitutional principles when a case could be decided without them. In *Patterson* all that was necessary was to rule that the contempt charge was in keeping with Colorado law and was therefore consistent and predictable.

Holmes could have stopped there. But in a telling moment of dicta, he added, "The main purpose of [the First Amendment] is 'to prevent all such *previous restraints* upon publications as had been practiced by other governments,' and they do not prevent the subsequent punishment of such as may be deemed contrary to the public welfare."[31] Taken in context with Holmes's earlier decisions in *Hanson v. Globe* and *Commonwealth v. Davis* on the Massachusetts Supreme Court, a pattern begins to emerge. Holmes looked to established precedent and common law rather than turning to the Constitution. Cases involving individual rights such as freedom of speech were not cause for exception. Holmes avoided constitutional issues by interpreting laws narrowly and with a presumption of constitutionality. Holmes believed the law should be upheld unless it was unconstitutional, but a law would only be judged unconstitutional if there was no way to interpret it otherwise. This decision-making methodology, or jurisprudence, gave a tremendous advantage to legislation and state action because it placed an overwhelming burden of proof on defendants to show the state had erred. Meanwhile, the Court began deliberations with the assumption that the state in fact had not erred and with the perceived duty of finding an interpretation of the law in question that would justify that presumption.

MOYER v. PEABODY. The individual rights at stake in this case, decided in 1909, were far different than those in *Patterson,* but again, Holmes's legal methodology gave preference to the state over the individual.[32] The governor of Colorado jailed a mine-workers' union leader when a strike turned violent. The Supreme Court appeal was not based upon the jailing itself, but on the claim that due process of law was denied the defendant when the governor and the Colorado courts refused to allow a speedy hearing to set bail.

Holmes dismissed any question of individual rights. Finding the state's actions acceptable, Holmes ruled that "what is due process of law depends on circumstances. It varies with the subject matter and the necessities of the situation."[33] Holmes reasoned the arrest was not a matter of punishment but a "good faith" and "honest" attempt to head off insurrection. The state had a right to protect itself. "Public danger," Holmes said, "warrants the substitution of executive process for judicial process."[34] Apparently, even Holmes's unbending belief in the need for predictability in law could fall if such were required to uphold the power of the state. The right of due process was in the Constitution. Holmes left it unexamined. The guiding principle was the power of the state and the presumption that the state acted in a constitutional manner.

BAILY v. ALABAMA. In this 1910 example involving individual rights Holmes dissented in order to uphold a statute rather than see it fall to a constitutional challenge.[35] This time it involved the Thirteenth Amendment prohibition against involuntary servitude.

A black plantation worker was prosecuted for fraud under Alabama law when he left his job before serving out the time period he had contracted to work. The Supreme Court majority found the law invalid because in practice it placed workers into involuntary servitude. The Court pointed out that the law was "peculiarly effective as against the poor and the ignorant, its most likely victims."[36]

Justice Holmes thought the Court went too far. He believed the majority used the pretense of the Constitution to examine the social ramifications of the act rather than sticking to the Court's business, the application of the act. The notion that the Thirteenth Amendment was violated because this was a southern law was anathema to Holmes. "Neither public document nor evidence," Holmes said, "disclose a law which by its administration is made something different from what it appears on its face, and therefore the fact that in Alabama it mainly concerns the blacks does not matter."[37] The case should have been decided the same whether the law originated in Alabama or New York, Holmes protested.

If the statute was a bad idea, then Holmes would leave it to the legislature to change the law. "If the contract is one that ought not to be made," Holmes said, "prohibit it. But if it is a perfectly fair and proper contract, I can see no reason why the State should not throw its weight on the side of performance."[38] Holmes refused to see the statute in terms of broad social ramifications. It simply punished "fraudulently obtaining money by a false pretense of an intent to keep the written contract in consideration of which . . . money is advanced."[39] To Holmes, the statute was constitutional on its face. The actual impact of the statute was none of the Court's business unless it could be shown the actual intent of the law was in itself unconstitutional.

The bottom line for Holmes remained the principle of avoiding constitutional interpretations by the Court by presuming constitutionality. The presence of a question of individual rights made no difference to the judicial outcome. "This was decided by the Supreme Court of Alabama," Holmes said, "and we should be bound by their construction of the statute, even if we thought it wrong. But I venture to add that I think it entirely right."[40]

FOX v. WASHINGTON. A newspaper sympathetic to a group of nudists was the focus of Holmes's attention in this 1915 case.[41] The facts of the case might suggest strong constitutional implications for freedom of expression. Holmes saw no more than the need to narrowly apply a statute. The case is one more example of Holmes's penchant to defer to the legislature and presume the constitutionality of its work.

A group called the "Homeites" was partial to nude sunbathing in the Washington woods. Their state of undress violated local law and after some arrests newspaper editor Jay Fox joined their cause in print. His editing resulted in a two-month jail sentence for violating another law — a statute that forbade printing, publishing or editing material designed to "encourage or advocate disrespect for law or any court or court of justice."[42] The material in question ran under the headline "The Nudes and the Prudes." The following are excerpts from the article:

"Eventually a few prudes got into the community and proceeded in the brutal, unneighborly way of the outside world to suppress the people's freedom." The article continued, "The well merited indignation of the people has been aroused." Finally, the article encouraged a boycott of those responsible for the "brutality" against the nudes "until these invaders will come to see the brutal mistake of their action and so inform the people."[43]

Fox claimed the charges against him violated his right of free speech through the Fourteenth Amendment. Holmes, however, turned to a familiar judicial logic. "So far as statutes fairly may be construed in such a way as to avoid doubtful constitutional questions they should be so construed," he said.[44] The job of the Supreme Court was not to look at a statute in a light that would define it as a violation of the Constitution. Just the opposite. The Court was to find a way to read the statute as constitutional. Holmes accomplished his task using the following logic: "It does not appear and is not likely that the statute will be construed to prevent publications merely because they tend to produce unfavorable opinions of a particular statute or of law in general. In this present case the disrespect for law that was encouraged was disregard of it — an overt breach and technically criminal act."[45]

Holmes gave the benefit of the doubt to the legislature and avoided the necessity of exploring in constitutional terms the impact of the statute in question. The authority of the state remained supreme.

There is a hint at the end of Holmes's *Fox* opinion that his personal sympathy was not really with the statute. After defending the power of the majority to enact such laws, Holmes said, "Of course we have nothing to do with the wisdom of the defendant, the prosecution, or the act. All that concerns us is that it cannot be said to infringe the Constitution of the United States."[46] Whatever Holmes's personal opinion of "The Nudes and the Prudes," his judicial opinion was predicated on a methodology that looked to the bare words of the statute and not to the statute's constitutional implications for freedom of expression.

HAMMER v. DAGENHART. This 1917 child labor law case involved federal legislation rather than state law.[47] Holmes dissented in this case and, although he ruled against the power of individual states in favor of the federal government, his dissent reflected a consistent pattern.

A congressional act prohibited the shipment across state lines of goods produced by child laborers. A five-member majority struck down the act as unconstitutional, ruling that Congress had no authority to regulate such practices. The Constitution gave Congress the power to regulate commerce. That did not include the power to regulate the manufacture of such goods.

Holmes had no such problems with the federal law. He read the statute to mean that a certain class of commerce was regulated: commerce composed of goods manufactured by children. Congress clearly had the power to regulate commerce between the states, and the fact that this act had an effect upon manufacturing was of no consequence. "But if an act is within the powers specifically conferred upon Congress, it seems to me that it is not made any less constitutional because of the inherent effects that it may have, however obvious it may be that it will have those effects, and that we are not at liberty upon such grounds to hold it void."[48]

Certainly Holmes believed in the power of each state to regulate itself. But such power must bend before the greater authority of the national government. "The public policy of the United States," Holmes said, "is shaped with a view to the benefit of the nation as a whole."[49] Some rights were reserved for the states. But just as Holmes read state statutes with the benefit of the doubt that kept them constitutional, he gave the same benefit of the doubt to federal legislation. Holmes did not question Congress's motives. The use of the commerce power "was for the consideration of Congress alone and . . . this court [has] always disavowed the right to intrude its judgment upon questions of policy or morals."[50]

Jurisprudence

The above cases suggest a consistent pattern in Justice Holmes's judicial actions. Holmes was keenly aware that the judiciary should operate within a narrowly defined parameter. Judicial decisions had to be tempered by methodological limits that ensured predictability in the law. Legislative law, and the Constitution itself, established those limits. A judge's duty was to uphold the majority rule. The constitutional doctrine of separation of powers did not allow the judiciary the freedom to second-guess the legislature in anything less than exceptional circumstances. The legitimate role of the courts was to use logic and deduction to ensure the consistent enforcement of the law, which in turn ensured predictability. Holmes's view of the judicial role required legislative deference. Statutes and acts were presumed constitutional.

When a defendant came before the bench, Justice Holmes did not see him as an individual. The legal question, not the specific circumstances of the defendant, was the issue upon which Holmes acted. In doing so Holmes could reassure himself and the Court that he was expounding the law and not a personal view of how society should act if it were up to him.

8

The Role of Law and the
Felt Necessities of the Time

And, in the problem before us—that of the First Amendment—
as we gather up the import of a series of opinions and decisions in
which, since 1919, the phrase 'clear and present danger,' has held
a dominating influence, I wish to argue that their effect upon our
understanding of self-government has been one of disaster.

ALEXANDER MEIKLEJOHN, 1948,
Political Freedom

P OLITICAL journal editor Max Eastman
told an audience in July 1917, "You can't
even collect your thoughts without getting
arrested for unlawful assemblage. They give you ninety days for
quoting the Declaration of Independence, six months for quoting the
Bible, and pretty soon somebody is going to get a life sentence for
quoting Woodrow Wilson in the wrong context."[1]

It was barely an overstatement. Herman Tucker worked for the
United States Forestry Service in 1909 in Missoula, Montana. Tucker
had no special interest in leftwing politics, and probably paid only
mild attention one day to a speaker on the street corner below his
second-story office. The speaker was a young logger and a Wobblie.
From his window Tucker could see the logger standing on a raised
platform and hear him reading from a familiar document. The
speech stopped when police arrested the logger and took him away.
Outraged, Tucker rushed outside to the now empty platform and

began to read from the logger's document. Tucker too was arrested for reading aloud from the Declaration of Independence.[2]

The three decades leading up to World War I were dangerous for anyone engaged in "un-American" activities. And the label seemed to fit almost anyone outside the mainstream. Free-speech scholar Nat Hentoff wrote in 1980, "This was a period during which such 'outsiders' as aliens, immigrants, workers trying to organize into unions, and political radicals served as primary targets for those, in and out of government, who were engaging in the grand old American hunt for 'un-Americans.' "[3]

Nationalism reached a piqued fever of hysteria during the war, despite the fact that there was never unanimous public support for entry into the European conflict. A law was passed in Nebraska making it a crime to teach German in the public schools.[4] There were rumors that German U-boats had landed spies. Red Cross supplies ready for shipment to the front had been sabotaged. The Bolsheviks were trying to corrupt the American social fabric by smuggling huge shipments of gold both into and out of the country. Little time or energy went into quelling overactive imaginations that led to the formation of citizen-action groups hunting enemy agents and searching for pockets of sedition. Official government policies added fuel to the witch-hunt fires. Thirty-five state legislatures enacted sedition laws in addition to the 1917 federal Espionage Act. By 1919, twenty-four states made it a crime to display a red flag. More than four thousand people were arrested by order of Woodrow Wilson's attorney general on a single January night in 1920. They were accused of being "communists."[5]

The 1917 arrest of Elizabeth Baer and Charles Schenck at the Philadelphia Socialist party headquarters, then, was not an isolated incident. The pair was caught in a web of nationalism and intolerance for free speech that dwarfed the 1798 Alien and Sedition Acts.

The new federal espionage and sedition legislation equipped the government to handle radicals such as Baer and Schenck. Congress passed laws that, in essence, made it a crime to *publicly* oppose the war. The executive branch, acting through the Justice Department, hunted for radicals, arrested them, and prosecuted them in court.

The Judgment

The antiradical fervor during the early decades of the twentieth century was in part the result of a phenomenon Oliver Wendell Holmes labeled years earlier as "the felt necessities of the time." "The life of the law," Holmes wrote in *The Common Law* in 1881, "has not been logic: it has been experience. The felt necessities of the time, prevalent moral and political theories, institutions of public policy . . . have had a great deal more to do than the syllogism in determining the rules by which men should be governed."6

Holmes had warned in "The Path of the Law" in 1887 against allowing moral values and political theories to intrude upon the judicial process. Yet, Holmes realized that elements outside the strict rule of law could and sometimes did influence judicial decision making. "Behind the logical form lies a judgment," Holmes said, "as to the relative worth and importance of competing legislative grounds, often an inarticulate and unconscious judgment, it is true, and yet the very root and nerve of the whole proceeding."7 Was the Court's ability to focus unemotionally on the rule of law in *Schenck* clouded even unconsciously by the prevalent public concerns and fears that infected the rest of the nation?

Few historians would suggest that Justice Holmes's opinion for the Court in *Schenck* simply ignored the teachings of the law to align with some personal perception of the public will, or even the public "good." Repeatedly, Holmes's judicial opinions prior to *Schenck* show a justice entrenched in the belief and the practice that political theories must be set aside in judicial decision making. Cases were decided by a rule of law, not by a vote of the majority of the public.

Holmes did believe strongly in the concept of majority rule, although that belief had a strong skeptical bent to it. "The first requirement of a sound body of law," Holmes wrote in *The Common Law*, "is that it should correspond with the actual feelings and demands of the community, whether right or wrong."8 Holmes did not put great stock, however, in the wisdom of the majority to make good law. "I am so skeptical as to our knowledge about the goodness or badness of laws that I have no practical criticism except what the crowd wants," Holmes wrote to Sir Frederick Pollock in 1910. "Personally I bet that the crowd if it knew more wouldn't want what it does—but that is immaterial."9 There is evidence that Holmes supported the war effort against the Germans and that he had little faith in Socialism. Writing to Lewis Einstein in the State Department in 1918, Holmes said, "I don't forget, as some seem to, that the Germans are not conquered yet."[10] Holmes summarized his feelings about Marxist theory to Einstein as "the emptiest humbug that ever served a red flag."[11] Yet Holmes was very aware that on the bench personal values had to be set aside. To Pollock he wrote, "Of course I enforce whatever constitutional laws Congress or anybody else sees fit to pass—but I don't disguise my belief that the Sherman Act is a humbug based on economic ignorance and incompetence."[12] The pattern is consistent in Holmes's personal and judicial writing. The justice may have considered a law to be based on "humbug" and the will of the majority to be foolish, but any such considerations were to be kept separate from professional judicial duty.

A Rule of Law Over Personal Belief

Once it is accepted that Holmes was forced by his own jurisprudence to base the *Schenck* decision on a rule of law rather than on public pressure or personal fancy, then the question becomes: On which rule of law did Holmes base his decision in *Schenck?* This question has received a dearth of discussion from historians and legal scholars. Instead, critics have contented themselves with analyses of Holmes's constitutional view of the First Amendment in *Schenck* without first determining the First Amendment's relative importance or weight in Holmes's judicial logic. Legal scholars Jerome Barron and Thomas Deines wrote, "The *Schenck* case . . . forced the Court to consider to what degree the First Amendment guarantees prohibiting abridgments on freedom of speech and press should be taken literally."[13] But was Holmes actually forced into that position in *Schenck?* Legal biographer H. N. Hirsch wrote in 1981, "Holmes' position on free speech . . . was ambiguous in the extreme. Holmes' court opinions on the subject can be read like tea leaves, taking out of them whatever position one seeks."[14]

If Holmes's *Schenck* opinion appears ambiguous to those concerned with First Amendment protections for freedom of expression, perhaps it is because the rule of law on which Holmes relied was something other than the familiar constitutional admonition, "Congress shall make no law."

Regrets

The Supreme Court had almost no First Amendment precedent of its own to turn to when it considered the *Schenck* briefs and oral arguments, met in conference to consider the case, and finally reached unanimous agreement on Holmes's opinion draft with his test of clear and present danger. The Court had never used the First Amendment to check the use or abuse of legislative authority.[15] One of Holmes's letters, sent to Harold Laski just days before the *Schenck* opinion was announced, suggests the justice was troubled by the case and that he was acutely aware of a difference between his personal opinion and his professional duty.

> At last I get a pause — all too late; though I had a little one in which I tucked in a book or two — but then came there a certain judge and asked me to take a case, one that I hoped the Chief would give me, but which wrapped itself around me like a snake in a deadly struggle to present the obviously proper in the forms of logic — the real substance being: Damn your eyes — that's the way 'it's' going to be.[16]

The letter suggests Holmes was sympathetic to upholding the defendants' right of free speech, but because of a rule of law — the "obviously proper" — upholding the convictions was "the way 'it's' going to be." Holmes was eager to take on the case — "one that I hoped the Chief would give me" — but he also was troubled by the implications of the situation that "wrapped itself around me like a snake in a deadly struggle." A letter written to Pollock two months later adds credence to this interpretation. Holmes complained that "fools, knaves and ignorant persons" were criticizing his Espionage Act decisions, insinuating that a defendant such as Schenck lost in Court "because he was a dangerous agitator and that obstructing the draft was just a pretense."[17] But Holmes hardly appeared to believe Schenck and others prosecuted under the Espionage Act were truly "dangerous agitators." He wrote to Pollock that April, "Now I hope the President will pardon him and some other poor devils with whom I have more sympathy. Those whose cases who have come before us have seemed poor fools whom I should have been inclined to pass over if I could. The greatest bores in the world are the come-outers who are cock-sure of a dozen nostrums. The dogmatism of a little education is hopeless."[18]

The crime in the Espionage Act cases, at least in Holmes's mind, was obstruction of the draft, a deed punishable under the Act, and the defendants were punished for violating the act, not for voicing their opinions. "There was a lot of jaw about free speech," Holmes told Pollock, "which I dealt with somewhat summarily in an earlier case — *Schenck v. U.S. . . .* and *Frohwerk v. U.S. . . .* As it happens I should go further probably than the majority in favor of it, and I daresay that it was partly on that account that the C. J. assigned the cases to me."[19]

Holmes appeared to be telling his friend Pollock that the First Amendment was a false issue in the Espionage Act decisions. The cases were based on the commission of a criminal act proscribed by Congress. Free speech was simply dealt with "summarily."

Holmes was troubled philosophically about the free speech element in the Espionage Act cases, but he was convinced that he must be guided in his decisions by a rule of law rather than a free speech philosophy. Writing to Laski about Schenck and other Espionage Act cases Holmes said, "I greatly regretted having to write them — and (between ourselves) that the Government pressed them to a hearing."[20] Once pressed, however, Holmes saw his judicial duty. "But on the only question before us," Holmes told Laski, "I could not doubt about the law. The federal judges seem to me (again between ourselves) to have got hysterical about the war. I should think the President when he gets through with his present amusements might do some pardoning."[21]

Laski replied two days later, "The point, I take it, is that to act otherwise would be to simply substitute judicial discretion for executive indiscretion with the presumption of knowledge against you. I think that you would agree that none of the accused ought to have been prosecuted; but since they have been and the statute is there, the only remedy lies in the field of pardon."[22]

Holmes wrote a similar justification for his Espionage Act case decisions to scholar Herbert Croly. "I cannot doubt," Holmes said, "that there was evidence warranting a conviction on the disputed issue of fact. Moreover I think the *clauses under consideration* not only were constitutional but were proper enough while the war was on."[23] Holmes told Croly that generally he favored "aeration of all effervescing convictions — there is no way so quick for letting them get flat."[24] Nevertheless, Congress had the right to prevent certain acts whether they were accomplished "by persuasion" or "by force."[25]

Holmes's letter to Croly was consistent with his jurisprudential approach. Sixteen years earlier in *Northern Securities Company v. United States,* Holmes wrote, "the statute must be construed in such a way as not merely to save its constitutionality but, so far as is consistent with a fair interpretation, not to raise grave doubts on that score."[26] In *Schenck,* the letter suggests, Holmes read the Espionage Act narrowly and found the "clauses under consideration" were constitutional. With the constitutional issue settled, the central question was whether "there was evidence warranting a conviction on the disputed issue of fact." The letter also suggests, however, that Holmes was not convinced that there was real danger in the speech that led eventually to prosecution under the Espionage Act. Nevertheless, even if such speech usually went "flat," the defendants' expressions were part of an action outlawed by Congress.

Justice Holmes operated under the tenet that his judicial duty required him to uphold the law, even if the specific law in question was not to his liking. His Espionage Act decisions in no way contradict this. Holmes summed up his jurisprudence well in a 1916 letter to Laski.

> The scope of state sovereignty is a question of fact. It asserts itself as omnipotent in the sense that what it sees fit to order it will make you obey. You may very well argue that it ought not to order certain things, and I agree. But if the government does see fit to order them . . . I conceive that order is as much law as any other—not merely from the point of view of the Court, which of course will obey it, but from any other rational point of view—if as would be the case, the government had the physical power to enforce its command. Law also as well as sovereignty is a fact.[27]

It is clear from his letters that Justice Holmes was aware of certain First Amendment considerations throughout the *Schenck* proceeding. But to what extent the First Amendment shaped the *Schenck* decision, and exactly what rule of law Holmes turned to, remains to be discussed.

9

The Rule of Law in *Schenck*

> In America a majority has enclosed thought within a formidable
> fence. A writer is free inside that area, but woe to the man who
> goes beyond it.
>
> ALEXIS DE TOCQUEVILLE, 1848

"I abhor, loathe and despise . . . long dis-
courses, and agree with Carducci the Ital-
ian poet who died some years ago," Justice
Holmes wrote in 1917, "that a man who takes half a page to say what
can be said in a sentence will be damned."[1] Holmes was true to
himself when he wrote the Court's opinion in *Schenck v. United States.*[2]
Despite the fact that Schenck was the Court's first ruling in an Espionage Act case, the justice's entire opinion required just over fifteen-
hundred words.

Holmes began with a summary of the indictments against Elizabeth Baer and Charles Schenck. The lower court found them guilty of
conspiracy to violate the Espionage Act, conspiracy to commit an
offense against the United States, and unlawful use of the mail.[3] The
defendants, Holmes wrote, "set up the First Amendment to the Constitution forbidding Congress to make any law abridging the freedom
of speech, or of the press, and bringing the case here on that ground
have argued some other points of which we must dispose."[4] The
defendants' "other points" constituted less than one-half of Holmes's
opinion in which the justice addressed three non–First Amendment
questions. Was there sufficient evidence to prove that Baer and
Schenck conspired to violate the Espionage Act? Was the evidence

seized under a search warrant admissible in court? Did the circulars in question actually constitute the commission of an illegal act? Each question required Holmes to make a judgment about a rule of law.

The Conspiracy

The question of sufficient evidence required a technical determination based on the accepted traditions and standards of law. "No reasonable man," Holmes said, "could doubt that the defendant Schenck was largely instrumental in sending the circulars about."[5] Holmes cited trial testimony that Schenck was general secretary of the Socialist party and was "in charge of the Socialist headquarters from which the documents were sent."[6] Schenck supervised the printing. Minutes from the August 13, 1917, Socialist meeting recorded that Schenck was "allowed $125 for sending the leaflets through the mail."[7]

"As to the defendant Baer," Holmes wrote, "there was evidence that she was a member of the Executive Board and that the minutes of its transactions were hers."[8] Holmes found the evidence sufficient "without going into confirmatory details that were proved" at the trial.[9]

"The argument as to the sufficiency of the evidence that the defendants conspired to send the documents," Holmes concluded, "only impairs the seriousness of the real defense."[10] The sufficiency question raised no constitutional dimensions. Justice Holmes's reference to the "seriousness of the real defense" chided the weakness of the first evidentiary point of law under contention. But if the real defense was the First Amendment argument Holmes referred to in his preceding paragraph as the grounds on which the case was brought, he was not yet ready to address that issue.

The Admissibility of Evidence

The second question, of the admissibility of the evidence seized under a search warrant, was technical and again required no First Amendment interpretations. Defense attorneys Gibbons and Nelson argued that because the defendants wrote some of

the documents gathered under a warrant to search the Socialist headquarters at 1326 Arch Street, using those documents as evidence
against them violated their constitutional rights. The argument was
based on the Fifth Amendment prohibition against self-incrimination
that states, "No person . . . shall be compelled in any criminal case to
be a witness against himself." The attorneys asked the Court to accept
the premise that the evidentiary use of the documents written by their
clients amounted to the same thing as forcing Baer and Schenck to
testify against themselves. The constitutional connection was tenuous
and the attorneys appeared to realize it as they couched their statement with qualifiers. "In theory, at least, the defendants maintain that
the Constitution was intended, in this respect, to prevent a prosecutor
from making a defendant testify against himself."[11]

The issue was a familiar element of criminal law, not an untried
theory on the frontier of constitutional adjudication. Justice Holmes
dismissed the argument in four sentences citing four cases as precedent.[12] The warrant was valid. Precedent clearly supported the finding that the evidence seized under the warrant was admissible. The
attempt to find a constitutional violation was "plainly unsound" and
merited no further comment from the justice.

Violation of the Espionage Act

The third question addressed whether in fact the defendants violated the Espionage Act when their antidraft circulars
were written and distributed. Holmes parried with the free speech
element as he answered the question, but it is important to note that
the justice saw a major distinction between whether the act was violated and whether the First Amendment made the act itself unconstitutional. The First Amendment component arose because the defendants' actions were in the form of speech. But the First Amendment
element was peripheral to deciding whether the defendants violated
the Espionage Act prohibition against "obstructing the recruiting and
enlistment service of the United States, when the United States was at
war with the German Empire."[13]

It was clear to Holmes the defendants conspired to violate the
act. "In impassioned language [the defendants' circular] intimated
that conscription was despotism in its worst form and a monstrous

wrong against humanity in the interest of Wall Street's chosen few," Holmes reiterated.[14] The circular said that people were duty-bound to oppose the draft. "Of course the document," Holmes reasoned, "would not have been sent unless it had been intended to have some effect, and we do not see what effect it could be expected to have upon persons subject to the draft except to influence them to obstruct the carrying of it out."[15]

Baer and Schenck did not argue the contention that they in fact wanted to disrupt the draft and Holmes noted the void in their argument. "The defendants do not deny," Holmes said, "that the jury might find against them on this point."[16]

Gibbons and Nelson did, however, attempt to raise a philosophical defense for their clients. "The defendants contend they are not criminals in the ordinary sense of the word," the attorneys said. "This is a political question. No matter what the law may be, no matter what even this high Court may decide, there is a question here of human freedom which will not down in spite of what the laws may say or what the laws may be."[17]

The defendants' reasoning presented a moral rather than a judicial question. Justice Holmes had considered the issue of morals and law twenty-two years earlier when he wrote, "Nothing but confusion of thought can result from assuming that the rights of a man in a moral sense are equally rights in the sense of the Constitution and the law."[18] The defendants admittedly looked for relief despite "what the laws may say or what the laws may be." Clearly it was not an argument Holmes could act on. Questions of public morality were for the legislature, not the courts. Holmes understood that individuals could find individual laws untenable. Nevertheless, the concept of law itself required obedience to the rules, and a major tenet of the law was the censure of acts unacceptable to the government. State sovereignty, Holmes had written to Harold Laski three years earlier, "asserts itself as omnipotent in the sense that what it sees fit to order it will make you obey."[19] Moral arguments were insufficient to prevent the Court from upholding the legislative will.

The tone of the defense arguments suggests the attorneys knew they were not on solid legal ground. Gibbons and Nelson argued "the right of free speech, if allowed fully, gives the right to persuade another to violate a law, since, legally, it is actually the one who violates the law who should be punished."[20] With no precedent to support such a claim, the attorneys said, "as the homely adage has it, 'you don't have to put your hand into the fire because I tell you to do so.' "[21]

Holmes's interest appeared to be piqued by the rationale the defense offered for its unique distinction between a person who persuades another to violate a law and the person who physically violates the law. "This is the distinction between words and acts," the Socialists' lawyers said.[22]

Speech As a Criminal Act

The concern with the distinction between words and acts was important. The First Amendment protected citizens from government interference with speech, but not from interference with illegal acts. If words could be viewed by the Court as an *act*, rather than as *speech*, the First Amendment would no longer be a central issue in the case. The question for the Court became: Can speech be considered an act?

"We admit that in many places and in ordinary times," Holmes wrote, "the defendants in saying all that was said in the circular would have been within their constitutional rights."[23] Holmes's words appear to be a First Amendment interpretation, but a counterinterpretation is suggested when Holmes's statement is placed within the context of his next sentence: "But the character of every act depends upon the circumstances in which it is done."[24] The first sentence offered a qualified protection for speech. Speech was protected "in many places and in ordinary times." But in the next sentence, without transition, the concept of speech disappeared and was replaced with "the character of every act." Holmes cited his fifteen-year-old opinion for the Court in *Aikens v. Wisconsin* for support.[25]

Aikens involved newspaper publishers, but was not a First Amendment or free speech case. Three publishers were accused of telling their advertising clients that if they submitted to an advertising rate hike at a fourth newspaper, similar rate hikes would be established at the other three papers. The publishers' pact to pressure advertisers violated a Wisconsin statute "prohibiting combinations for the purpose of wilfully or maliciously injuring another in his . . . trade, business or profession."[26]

When Holmes cited *Aikens* he removed his judicial methodology from the realm of First Amendment interpretation and placed it into the more familiar arena of deduction based on general legal principles and case-law precedent. *Aikens* had nothing to do with free speech. Yet, Holmes reasoned that, logically, if not substantively, *Aikens* and *Schenck* carried parallel implications for deciding a case. Holmes's jurisprudence was not unique. Deductive reasoning is the bulwark of judicial decision making. The legal reasoning of past cases, rather than the identical fact situations, were and still are used to deduce the proper legal rule.[27] Holmes had used the concept of deciding cases from general principles established in earlier decisions in his 1881 treatise, *The Common Law.*

Holmes's reference to *Aikens* involved a long, but important passage.

> But an act, which in itself is merely a voluntary muscular contraction, derives all its character from the consequences which will follow it under the circumstances in which it was done. When the acts consist of making a combination calculated to cause temporal damage, the power to punish such acts, when done maliciously, cannot be denied because they are to be followed and worked out by conduct which might have been lawful if not preceded by the acts. No conduct has such an absolute privilege as to justify all possible schemes of which it may be a part. The most innocent and constitutionally protected of acts or omissions may be made a step in a criminal plot, and if it is a step in a plot neither its innocence nor the Constitution is sufficient to prevent the punishment of the plot by law.[28]

No speech element was present in *Aikens,* yet the legal principle was applicable to *Schenck.* Normally people may "combine." Normally people may "speak freely." But the character and circumstances of the act, not the abstract combination or speech, determined the proper legal rule to be applied. Holmes had no need to risk a constitutional confrontation. The proper legal rule and the resolution of *Schenck* could be deduced from the general legal principle set down in *Aikens.*

Justice Holmes's next five sentences are perhaps his most remembered utterances from *Schenck.*

> The most stringent protection of free speech would not protect a man in falsely shouting fire in a theater and

causing a panic. It does not even protect a man from an injunction against uttering words that may have all the effect of force. *Gompers v. Buck Stove and Range Co.*, 221 U.S. 418, 439. The question in every case is whether the words are used in such circumstances and are of such a nature as to create a clear and present danger that they will bring about the substantive evils that Congress has a right to prevent. It is a question of proximity and degree. When a nation is at war many things that might be said in time of peace are such a hindrance to its effort that their utterance will not be endured so long as men fight and that no Court could regard them as protected by any constitutional right.[29]

These lines have proved the most troubling for those interested in the First Amendment. They establish an exception to the constitutional admonition against congressional interference with speech. When words create a "clear and present danger" during a time of war they cannot be "endured" or "protected by any constitutional right." Congress, despite the commands of the Constitution, created a law abridging speech. The Court refused to lay the Constitution in the path of Congress' lawmaking.

Holmes's clear and present danger doctrine appeared to have all the attributes of a judicial constitutional interpretation. It established a judicial test to determine the circumstances under which speech may be abridged. But an examination of Holmes's jurisprudence — the methodological process he followed to construct the clear and present danger test — indicates far more attention to criminal law precedent and generalized principles than to a carefully reasoned interpretation of the First Amendment.

Holmes's fire-in-a-theater metaphor was neither law nor legal philosophy. It was an example intended to clarify a phrase for which Holmes had in mind a technical legal definition: "uttering words that may have all the effect of force." The notion of words as one and the same as actions because of effect does not come from the Constitution, but from *Gompers v. Buck Stove and Range Co.*, a 1910 case that dealt with a boycott.[30] Labor leader Samuel Gompers was held in contempt for violating an injunction restraining him and others from a boycott or "publishing any statement that there was or had been a boycott" against the stove company.

Gompers argued that his circular, which in fact encouraged a boycott, was protected by the First Amendment. In an unsigned opinion that paralleled and precursored some of the logic in *Schenck* the Court ruled that an act, rather than speech, was the issue before the Court. "Under such circumstances," the Court said, "[words] become what [have] been called 'verbal acts,' as much subject to injunction as the use of any other force whereby property is unlawfully damaged."[31]

Gompers provided precedent for Holmes that words and acts could be one in the same. "The strong current of authority," the Court had announced nine years prior to *Schenck*, "is that the publication and use of letters, circulars and printed matter may constitute a means whereby a boycott is unlawfully continued, and their use for such purposes may amount to a violation of the order of injunction."[32] The *Gompers* Court cited fifteen cases as authority. Again, Holmes had no need to chart new constitutional territory in *Schenck*. The precedent was there for the taking.

The first four of Holmes's five-sentence clear and present danger doctrine simply applied a variation on the theme set by precedent found in case law such as *Gompers* and *Aikens* — a word can be an act and Congress has the authority to prohibit certain acts. The fifth sentence returned, tangentially, to the Constitution. "When a nation is at war many things that might be said in time of peace are such a hindrance to its effort that their utterance will not be endured so long as men fight and that no Court could regard them as protected by any constitutional right."[33] This is not, however, an explanation of the First Amendment. It is a conclusion. The logic behind it was deduced from precedent. Holmes never addressed the core of the constitutional issue as it related to the First Amendment.

The interpretation offered here of Holmes's judicial reasoning in *Schenck* suggests the justice's conclusions were based on deduction from case law precedent, statutory interpretation, and the record of trial testimony and physical evidence. Table 9.1 summarizes the deductions that Holmes appeared to make.

TABLE 9.1   *Summary of Holmes's Deduction in Schenck*

ASSUMPTION/CONCLUSION	LEGAL METHODOLOGY
A. Baer and Schenck were responsible for certain words.	A. Testimony and physical evidence.
B. Defendants intended the words to have a certain effect.	B. Testimony and physical evidence.
C. Words intended to have an effect or having an effect are acts rather than speech.	C. Case law precedent.
D. Defendants' words were acts rather than speech.	D. Deduced from A, B, and C.
E. Espionage Act prohibits certain acts.	E. Statutory interpretation.
F. First Amendment does not prohibit Congress from outlawing certain acts.	F. Constitutional interpretation.
G. Defendants' words were an act prohibited by law.	G. Deduced from A, B, C, D, E, and F.
H. Therefore, defendants' words were prohibited by Espionage Act.	H. Deduced from A, B, C, D, E, F, and G.
I. Therefore, some words deserve no First Amendment protection.	I. Deduced from G.

The First Amendment

The First Amendment had little if any importance in deciding the evidentiary issues in *Schenck.* But the constitutional prohibition against interfering with speech was at the heart of the defendants' defense strategy. Unfortunately for Baer and Schenck, their attorneys presented weak arguments. Gibbons and Nelson substituted political rhetoric and generalities for substantive legal doctrine and established precedent.

"If all opponents of war," the attorneys said, "are suppressed and all advocates of a war are given free rein, is it not conceivable that a peace-loving president might be prevented from making an early, honorable peace, founded on justice! How can the citizens find out whether a war is just or unjust unless there is free and full discussion."[34]

The defendants' question was ideological and its rhetorical nature made it incapable of eliciting a substantive legal response. Nevertheless, the attorneys continued their First Amendment probe. "Are we Americans big enough to allow honest criticism of the majority by the minority! In days gone by it was held criminal to talk against flogging in the army; nowadays it is generally considered criminal to talk against Wall Street."[35] Each query was followed by an exclamation point rather than a question mark.

Finally, Gibbons and Nelson postulated what they saw as a judicial test to determine the limits of First Amendment protection.

"It would seem," they wrote, "that the fair test of protection by the constitutional guarantee of free speech is whether expression is made with sincere purpose to communicate honest opinion or belief, or whether it masks a primary intent to incite to forbidden action, or whether it does, in fact, incite to forbidden action."[36]

The proposed test, like the other arguments the defense presented, offered little protection from the Espionage Act. Here the defense seemed to admit that the "intent to incite to forbidden action" was sufficient grounds to nullify First Amendment protections. Yet before the attorneys wrote their test, the trial court had ruled that Baer and Schenck were trying to convince draft-age men to refuse the draft — clearly an intent to incite to forbidden action.

Holmes never mentioned the attorneys' "test" in his opinion. Instead, the justice developed his own question. If the "tendency of the circular" was in fact to obstruct the draft, was the circular still "protected by the First Amendment to the Constitution?"[37]

Holmes gave no ground. Referring for the first time directly to the First Amendment, Holmes said, "It well may be that the prohibition of laws abridging the freedom of speech is not confined to previous restraints, although to prevent them may have been the main purpose, as intimated in *Patterson v. Colorado*."[38] The sentence is a contradiction and does nothing to illuminate the meaning of the First Amendment. On the one hand Holmes admits the framers' "main purpose" may have been to prohibit prior restraints on speech, a conclusion he reached twelve years earlier in *Patterson v. Colorado*. In the same breath, however, Holmes suggested "the prohibition of laws abridging freedom of speech is not confined to previous restraints." It cannot be both ways. Yet Holmes quit there and provided no further discussion relevant to the legal definition of the First Amendment. In context, it appears that Holmes, more than addressing the First Amendment, was actually responding to a somewhat disjointed portion of the defense brief. Gibbons and Nelson had argued that "in general, our courts have held that the free speech and free press amendment applies to freedom from interference 'before' publication. The Espionage Act only imposes punishment 'after' publication."[39] The point was a strange one for the defense to raise since Baer and Schenck were indeed being punished after publication, not before. The defense may have hoped to create a new theory of First Amendment application.

"But how," Gibbons and Nelson asked, "can a speaker or writer be said to be free to discuss the actions of the Government if twenty years in prison stares him in the face if he makes a mistake and says too much? Severe punishment for sedition will stop political discussion as effectively as censorship."[40]

Holmes did not answer the defendants' question. At best, the justice's reference to *Patterson* acknowledged the query—hardly a signal that the authoritative meaning of the First Amendment was "the seriousness of the real defense" Holmes promised to address. The conclusion to be reached is that Holmes gave little serious consideration in Schenck to the First Amendment. Support for this interpretation comes not only from Holmes's relative lack of direct reference to the amendment in his opinion, but also from Holmes's statement a few weeks later to Sir Edward Pollock. "There was a lot of jaw about free speech," Holmes said, "which I wrote about somewhat summarily."[41]

In essence, Holmes reached a conclusion that had a direct bearing upon the First Amendment without providing a serious discussion of the First Amendment prohibition against the abridgment of speech. Holmes never explained *why* the First Amendment allows speech to be abridged. He only explained when speech may be abridged. Everything else consisted of non–First Amendment interpretation.

The effect of Holmes's conclusion, nevertheless, was not a congressional license to abridge speech. Holmes said, in essence, that Congress could prohibit an *act* that occurred in the guise of speech.

What Holmes did not take into account was that in abridging such acts, Congress automatically interferes with speech because the abridged acts are speech.

The Act, Tendency and Intent

Justice Holmes was satisfied that words that in fact obstructed military enlistment were proscribed by the Espionage Act. "It seems to be admitted," Holmes wrote, "that if an actual obstruction of the military service were proved, liability for words that produced that effect might be enforced."[42] This was not a First Amendment interpretation, but a reading of the statute that assigned liability for words producing an effect. Holmes continued on this track. It did not even matter whether the words in question actually had an effect. "If the act, (speaking, or circulating a paper) its tendency and the intent with which it is done are the same, we perceive no ground for saying that success alone warrants making the act a crime."[43]

The idea was not a new one. Holmes cited *Goldman v. United States* for support, a two-year-old case that had emphasized the legal doctrine that the intent to commit a crime is punishable whether or not the intended illegal act is carried to fruition.[44] Again the justice found his legal reasoning in case law and could avoid the need to directly interpret the Constitution. And again, *Goldman*, like *Aikens*, provided precedent for *Schenck* from a case devoid of First Amendment issues. In essence, *Goldman* was a conspiracy case in which Chief Justice Edward White reiterated the well-established legal principle that a conspiracy to commit a crime "is in and of itself inherently and substantively a crime punishable as such irrespective of whether the result of the conspiracy has been to accomplish the illegal end."[45]

Holmes's original justification in *Schenck* for excluding certain words from First Amendment protection, however, was that the words might have "all the effect of force."[46] The assumption was that words with the effect of force inherently became an act in the eyes of the law. Yet, now Holmes borrowed a general legal principle from *Goldman* and stated, "there was no ground for saying that success alone warrants making the act a crime." If the intended effect of the words was unsuccessful, then the only way to continue to perceive the words as an act was to focus on the defendants' intent rather than on the effect of the words. It is one thing to say that a conspiracy to commit a crime is a crime whether or not the conspiracy is successful, and quite another to extend that logic to the premise that words are an act whether or not the words produce their intended effect. However, that is precisely the logic Holmes carried from *Goldman* to *Schenck,* and it appears to be an admission by Holmes that Schenck's circulars did not have the force of "a man falsely shouting fire in a theater and causing a panic."[47] No substantive proof was offered in *Schenck* that the character of the circular and the circumstances in which it was published created a "clear and present danger that [would] bring about the substantive evils that Congress had a right to prevent."[48] Substantive evils are an effect. Holmes's logic in *Schenck* was based on the premise that the speech in question was an act, and the inherent deduction that speech, as an act, may be punished. Holmes's judicial logic is greatly weakened by the conclusion that the speech need not be successful to be punished. Without success the words have no force of effect and without effect Holmes's own examples, such as shouting fire in a theater and causing a panic, are ill-fitted to the actual circumstances surrounding *Schenck.*

Holmes weakened his own clear and present danger doctrine and broadened the circumstances under which constitutional protection for speech may be denied. Yet the justice relied on brief references to non–First Amendment case-law precedents from which he deduced a rule directly affecting freedom of speech.

"Indeed," Holmes said, "[*Goldman*] might be said to dispose of the present contention if the precedent covers all 'media concludendi.' But as the right to free speech was not referred to specifically, we have thought fit to add a few words."[49] Holmes seemed to suggest in these two sentences that he had not simply relied on *Goldman,* but had adequately discussed the free speech implications as well. The justice supplied nothing more in his opinion on free speech or the First Amendment.

Recruiting Volunteers

The final paragraph of Holmes's *Schenck* opinion interpreted the legislative intent of a single phrase of the Espionage Act.

The words "obstruct the recruiting or enlistment service" held a broad meaning, Holmes ruled. The words did not "refer only to making it hard to get volunteers."[50] Finally, Holmes added, "The fact that the Act of 1917 was enlarged by the Amending Act of May 16, 1918, c.75, 40 Stat. 553, of course, does not affect the present indictment and would not, even if the former act had been repealed."[51]

The judgments against Baer and Schenck were affirmed by a unanimous Court.

Statutory v. Constitutional Law

We have suggested that Holmes's judicial methodology was flawed because it avoided the underlying First Amendment issues in the case, despite Holmes's admission in the first paragraph of his opinion that the case was brought to the Court on First Amendment grounds. *Schenck* provided the opportunity for a careful discussion of the First Amendment. Why is speech protected by the Constitution? What are the dangers of prohibiting speech critical of governmental policies? Holmes avoided these issues and settled for the formulation of the clear and present danger doctrine.

Justice Holmes considered narrow legal questions in *Schenck*.

Was there sufficient evidence to convict the defendants? Yes, the record of trial testimony and physical evidence made it clear there was.

Was the evidence admissible that was seized under a search warrant? Yes, non–First Amendment case-law precedent supported that finding and the defense offered no substantive arguments to the contrary.

Did the defendants' circular fall within the category of acts prohibited by the Espionage Act? Yes, a statutory interpretation of the act showed this to be the case.

Each question was an important issue in the resolution of *Schenck v. United States* and none required First Amendment interpretation. The First Amendment component grew out of the answer to the third question. If the Espionage Act outlawed Schenck's circular, did the act violate the First Amendment because the circular was a form of speech normally protected? The circular was not protected because it was an act rather than speech, a finding made possible by deductive reasoning and precedent that barely gave notice to the First Amendment.

The conclusion to be drawn from an analysis of *Schenck* is that the case dealt far more with procedural matters and statutory interpretations than with the First Amendment.

This does not mean that the First Amendment was not part of the *Schenck* decision. Holmes's opinion inherently involved the First Amendment because it established a judicial test applicable to free-speech sedition cases. And the case is important to those interested in the First Amendment because the Court allowed speech to be abridged. Those interested in the First Amendment, however, should keep in mind the manner in which *Schenck* was settled. There is a distinction between cases that contain important First Amendment concerns and cases that are decided by legal methodologies deeply rooted in the First Amendment.

10

A Clear and Present Danger

> Everywhere today men are conscious that somehow they must
> deal with questions more intricate than any that church or school
> had prepared them to understand. Increasingly they know that
> they cannot understand them if the facts are not quickly and
> steadily available. Increasingly they are baffled because the facts
> are not available; and they are wondering whether government
> by consent can survive in a time when the manufacture of con-
> sent is an unregulated private enterprise.
>
> WALTER LIPPMANN, 1919
> *Liberty and the News*

JUSTICE Oliver Wendell Holmes's opinion for
the unanimous Court was released March 3,
1919. The *Washington Post* headlined its coverage
the next day:

SUSTAINS "SPY" LAW

Supreme Court Upholds Several
Convictions in Lower Courts

The *New York Times* headline proclaimed:

SUPREME COURT RULES
AGAINST PACIFISTS

Holds Enlistment Section of Espionage
Act No Interference
with "Free Speech"

Identical lead paragraphs of the *Times* and *Post* informed readers that "while not passing directly upon the question of the constitutionality of the espionage act, the Supreme Court in disposing of proceedings involving an interpretation of that statute yesterday, in effect, held that the so-called enlistment section is not an interference with the right of free speech provided by the Constitution."[1]

Evidence suggests that the First Amendment played only a minor role in Justice Holmes's opinion in *Schenck v. United States*. But whether or not agreement ultimately can be reached as to the degree to which Holmes relied on the first amendment upholding the sedition convictions against Elizabeth Baer and Charles Schenck, his opinion for the United States Supreme Court provides some valuable lessons.

"Even if it be agreed that the 'clear and present danger' formula denies rather than expresses the meaning of the Constitution," Alexander Meiklejohn wrote in 1948, "even if we are convinced that the guarantee of freedom of public discussion which is provided by the First Amendment admits of no exceptions, we are, because of those very conclusions, plunged at once into a multitude of bewildering questions."[2]

Supreme Court historian Leo Pfeffer approached his bewilderment with historical context predating *Schenck* by more than a century. "The clear and present danger test has been widely hailed as a great, libertarian contribution to civil rights. Yet it should be noted that actually it represented a retreat. . . . According to the Holmes formula, civil government could rightfully interfere where there was a clear and present danger that overt acts would break out, even though they have not yet done so.[3]

The purpose of this examination of Holmes's jurisprudence in *Schenck* was not to find the ultimate meaning of the constitutional prohibition against congressional interference with freedom of expression. Three questions were formulated in the first chapter. Is there reason to suspect that Justice Holmes did not base his opinion in *Schenck* on the First Amendment? Is there an alternative to the thesis that Holmes based his decision on the First Amendment? And finally, what is the relation of the specific intricacies of the American judicial system to any consideration of laws that may have an impact upon a citizen's freedom of speech?

The Absence of the First Amendment

Three findings led to the conclusion that the First Amendment played a minimal role in Justice Holmes's *Schenck* decision.

The most important evidence is Holmes's opinion itself. The justice concentrated on answering questions that involved technical rules, evidentiary considerations, and statutory interpretations. Holmes found sufficient evidence that Baer and Schenck conspired to violate provisions of the 1917 Espionage Act. He ruled that evidence seized under a search warrant was admissible in court. He agreed that Baer and Schenck violated the Espionage Act by their intention to obstruct the draft. And Holmes interpreted the scope of the Espionage Act in terms of what he saw as the legislative intent behind the act and the act's relation to its 1918 amendment.

Justice Holmes spent almost no time in his opinion interpreting the meaning of the First Amendment. In a short passage he referred to the intentions of the framers of the Bill of Rights and said that their purpose may have been to prevent prior restraints on speech. In the same sentence, however, Holmes added that "it may well be that the prohibition of laws abridging the freedom of speech is not confined to previous restraints."[4] Holmes did not develop the discussion any further. His clear and present danger doctrine explained when speech could be abridged but his explanation was a conclusion about the First Amendment, not an analysis of its meaning. Holmes did not discuss the free speech implications of either the Espionage Act or the clear and present danger doctrine and he omitted any explanation of why the First Amendment allowed speech to be abridged.

Justice Holmes's letters to Pollock and Croly provide a second level of evidence that the First Amendment was not an important judicial element in *Schenck*. In these he determined that issues of fact belong in the category of evidentiary and statutory consideration, not constitutional adjudication.[5]

Finally, the analysis of Holmes's writing off the bench and his judicial style in cases prior to *Schenck* identify a consistent pattern. Holmes did not view the courtroom as a forum to criticize legislation. He was skeptical about the public's understanding of important national issues and the ability of legislatures to pass wise laws. But

Holmes's skepticism did not interfere with his notion of the judicial role.

Justice Holmes's conception of the rule of law, his understanding of the constitutionally mandated separation of powers between the legislature and the judiciary, and his strong belief in upholding the will of the majority combined to form an almost inviolate code of judicial behavior. Given the choice between ruling on the application of a statute or on the constitutionality of that statute, Holmes invariably chose the former. "[Statutes] must be construed in such a way," Holmes wrote in 1903, "as not merely to save [their] constitutionality but, so far as is consistent with a fair interpretation, not to raise grave doubts on that score."[6]

Holmes believed that laws were to be upheld unless they were unconstitutional and that the burden of proof to show a constitutional violation fell upon the defendant. Meanwhile, Holmes began judicial deliberations with the assumption that not only was the statute in question constitutional, but that it was the Court's role to look for an interpretation of the law in question that would justify that presumption.

The role of the judiciary was clear to Holmes. The courts' task was to uphold legislation and to bring the force of the state, through the instrument of the courts, down upon anyone who violated a law.

Justice Holmes's behavior was consistent with the history and traditions of the Court in 1919. Courtroom actions such as judicial review that challenged the integrity of legislative enactments carried dangerous risks. Overruling legislatures could always be perceived by critics as an illegitimate use of judicial power, as was the case for Chief Justice Roger Taney in *Dred Scott v. Sanford.*[7] Holmes was not prepared, either by his personal conception of the judicial role or by the contemporary practices of the judiciary to take such risks lightly.

Taken in context with the practices of the Court and Holmes's personal notion of the judicial role, it would have been surprising if the justice had attempted to shield Baer and Schenck from the legislative will represented by the Espionage Act by turning to the First Amendment to challenge the application and constitutionality of the act.

First Amendment Alternatives

The second question asked whether there is an alternative to the thesis that Holmes based his *Schenck* decision on the First Amendment. Obviously the questions involving the admissibility and sufficiency of evidence were not First Amendment issues. *Schenck* did raise the inherent question, however, of whether the First Amendment shielded the defendants' speech from prosecution put into motion by a congressional act.

Holmes used deductions based on non–First Amendment precedent to remove the question from the constitutional arena. In essence, Holmes did not ask whether speech was protected by the First Amendment, but whether speech could be treated as an act. This was more than a semantic difference. If the actions of Baer and Schenck violated the Espionage Act there was nothing in the Constitution to protect them. Holmes assumed that the antidraft circular was in fact an action rather than speech. He cited case-law precedent involving a statute prohibiting combinations to injure another's business and a contempt of court case to build the nexus between speech and action. Holmes did not treat the abridgment of speech as a unique legal question. The argument today can be raised that Holmes should have examined the application of the Espionage Act to Baer and Schenck within the strict context of the First Amendment prohibition against the abridgment of freedom of speech. But Holmes did not. The impact of the First Amendment was lost in *Schenck* because Holmes applied the logic of past nonspeech cases to his judicial reasoning. Holmes was unwilling or unable to see the speech component of *Schenck* as a unique issue. Today a speech component may distinguish judicial considerations from the decision-making procedures applied to other criminal cases. But the Court had little experience to draw on in speech cases in 1919, and there was no Supreme Court precedent that successfully challenged an abridgment of speech as unconstitutional.

The Law and Freedom of Expression

The final question asked how the specific intricacies of the American judicial system impact upon a citizen's right to freedom of speech. *Schenck* provides a specific answer based on a specific example. But the lessons of *Schenck* can be generalized.

The Espionage Act facilitated the prosecution of people who disagreed with the policies of the government and put their beliefs into words. The First Amendment would seem inherently involved in any circumstance in which the government prosecutes individuals for the words they speak. But the Court's jurisprudence in *Schenck* made it possible and perhaps inevitable that First Amendment considerations would be glossed over. *Schenck* was decided on non–First Amendment grounds because the decision-making procedures available and familiar to Justice Holmes and the Court neither required a thorough consideration of First Amendment theory nor made it desirable to consider the full complexities of the relation of the First Amendment to judicial proceedings. The Court saw *Schenck* as a criminal case in which two defendants were prosecuted for violating a statute. The taught traditions of the law and the need to remain within the traditional axioms of judicial conduct dictated that the *Schenck* Court would take a conservative approach.

The *Schenck* decision is a better example of jurisprudence in 1919 than of Holmes's beliefs about freedom of speech. Holmes did not develop a comprehensive interpretation of the First Amendment in *Schenck* because he did not have to do so to settle the legal dispute and because doing so would have been out of step with accepted judicial practices.

The lesson from *Schenck* for those concerned with First Amendment guarantees of freedom of expression is a lesson of context. Every instance of repression that abridges the free discussion of ideas can be viewed by the public as an attack on the First Amendment. But the First Amendment view will not always be the primary legal concern of the courts. Judges may be confronted with circumstances involving freedom of speech and see only legal questions that involve statutory interpretations, the law of contracts, or any of a dozen other non–First Amendment questions of law. The presence of issues that involve the freedom of speech does not guarantee in any way that those issues will be the legal questions on which a judge believes a case must be decided.

The legal context in which attacks on the freedom of expression appear and the identification of the specific legal questions involved will determine in great part the legal response to those attacks. The situation was frustrated in *Schenck* because the attorneys for Baer and Schenck provided a weak defense. They argued the case poorly and presented few if any substantive legal issues capable of acceptance by the Court.

The conclusion to be reached from *Schenck* is that people who are concerned with the First Amendment must be concerned with more than First Amendment theory and philosophy. Those interested in the freedom of speech must understand more than the notion that the unabated dissemination of ideas is the basis of democracy. It is just as important to understand the legal context within which the First Amendment operates. Historians, legal scholars and civil libertarians are in a far better position to defend the rights guaranteed by the First Amendment when they understand how the First Amendment operates within the American legal system as well as the philosophical tenets upon which democratic governance is founded.

The record is barren about what happened to Elizabeth Baer and Charles Schenck after 1919, although immediately after the Armistice the president commuted at least 103 prison sentences that had been based on the Espionage Act and similar legislation. The 1917 Espionage Act and its 1918 Sedition Amendment, like their 1798 prototype, expired, unrenewed by Congress, in 1921.

Bombs For the Justice

At two o'clock in the morning, May Day, 1919, Charles Caplan began his walk home from work, the Parcel Post division of the Post Office, in New York. A newspaper article caught the Harlem resident's attention. A bomb had gone off at the Atlanta, Georgia, home of Senator Thomas Hardwick. The senator was not at home. His wife suffered severe burns, and the maid lost both hands in the explosion. It was the details of the incident, however, that troubled Caplan.

The article described the small package in which the bomb, wrapped in brown paper, had arrived through the mails at the senator's house. There were sixteen packages that matched just that description in the Parcel Post Division storage room at the Post Office where Caplan worked at Thirty-third Street and Eighth Avenue. The packages had been set aside, undelivered, because of a postage problem. They were sealed with red stickers and the sealing made them first class. Additional postage was due before they would be delivered.

Caplan reported his observations to authorities who discovered thirty-six bombs in all. The intended victims included Supreme Court Justice Oliver Wendell Holmes, Attorney General A. Mitchell Palmer, John D. Rockefeller, J. P. Morgan, and Ole Hanson, the mayor of Seattle. Hanson's package was found at his home. Fourteen of the bombs were found in post offices on the Pacific coast.[8]

Suspicion turned immediately in the direction of the political left. The *Times* reported that "the [Industrial Workers of the World] I.W.W.-Bolsheviki suspicion entertained by the Federal and local authorities is strengthened because of the activities of some of the men to whom the bombs were mailed."[9] Many, like Holmes, had been involved with the enforcement of statutes used against labor movements, socialists, and pacifists.

The bombing attempts made for good theater. The following day the newspapers reported the discovery of still more bombs as officials warned of a national conspiracy.[10] With new revelations each day, federal officials compiled a list of two-hundred "radicals" and "troublemakers" in New York City deserving of close scrutiny. By the end of the second week the deck of *Times* headlines reported,[11]

POLICE ASK HELP TO
FIND BOMB SENDERS

Enright Issues Offer of Reward
After Department Fails to
Develop Clues

FEDERAL AGENTS ARE BUSY

Government Sleuths, It Is Said, Are
Sifting Several Leads That
Promise Results Shortly

The hoped-for results never came, despite enormous efforts by
federal agents. Secretary of Labor Louis Post, however, questioned
the motives behind the investigations and wondered aloud in a 1923
narrative whether the bombs were actually the work of the left. "Only
one conclusion, not a flattering one, seems possible," Post wrote,
"when the facilities of the detectives of the Justice Department are
considered."[12] The Attorney General's staff collected dossiers on two
hundred thousand "ultra-radicals," as well as myriad organizations
and publications. "When it is considered that not withstanding all the
kaiseristic police mechanism[s] . . . no disclosure whatever has yet
been made of any responsibility . . . what inference is possible, in all
reason, except that the crimes were not of 'ultra-radical' origin, or else
that the detectives were grossly inefficient?"[13]

Whether or not the bombs were truly planted by radicals or the
work of rightest provocateurs, the climate after the war was hardly
improved for individuals who wished to voice ideas out of the mainstream.

From Majority to Minority

For Holmes, however, something was indeed chang-
ing. Exactly one week after the *Schenck* opinion was handed down,
Holmes authored two more opinions for the Court based on the
Espionage and Sedition Acts. These marked the last time the justice
agreed with the Court's approach to abridgments of freedom of
speech.

In *Frohwerk v. United States* Holmes upheld the appealed convictions under the acts.[14] Again, the defendants had written antiwar
sentiments, this time in a newspaper. Again, Bettman and O'Brian
were the prosecutors. Holmes pointed to *Schenck* as precedent, but
wondered whether more evidence at the trial level would not have
suggested that there had been no clear and present danger.

> It may be that all this might be said or written even in time
> of war in circumstances that would not make it a crime.
> We do not lose our right to condemn either measures or
> men because the Country is at war. It does not appear that
> there was any special effort to reach men who were subject
> to the draft. . . . But we must take the case on the record

as it is, and on that record it is impossible to say that it might not have been found that the circulation of the paper was in quarters where a little breath would be enough to kindle a flame and that the fact was known and relied upon by those who sent the paper out.[15]

Blocked by a jurisprudence that did not allow consideration of issues not in the trial record—such as the lack of evidence at the trial of a clear and present danger—Holmes could only rule on the violation of the statute.

Debs v. United States was decided the same day.[16] The familiar team of Bettman and O'Brian charged well-known socialist Eugene Debs with violation of the Espionage Act and the Sedition amendment. Debs responded that he had a First Amendment right to express his views. He had, in fact, told the jury at his trial, "I have been accused of obstructing the war. I admit it. Gentlemen, I abhor war. I would oppose the war if I stood alone."[17] Holmes dismissed Deb's First Amendment claim. "The chief defenses upon which the defendant seemed willing to rely . . . based upon the First Amendment," Holmes wrote for the unanimous Court, "[was] disposed of in *Schenck*."[18] Holmes was willing to accept a clear and present danger in Deb's socialism and in his pacifist efforts. Again, the question was whether the statute was violated. The constitutional dimensions of *Debs* were small and already were dealt with in *Schenck*.

A trio of cases rounded out Holmes's participation in Espionage Act cases. They marked an important change for the jurist. In *Abrams v. United States, Schaefer v. United States,* and *Pierce v. United States* Holmes could not go along with the majority to uphold prison terms for seditious speech.[19] Holmes joined with dissents written by Brandeis in the latter two cases. He wrote what may have been his finest statements on freedom of speech in *Abrams*.

It is not clear what brought on Holmes's change of heart, if indeed that is what it was.[20] Nonetheless, after a summer recess, the Court found itself divided for the first time on a case of sedition. Holmes, joined in dissent by Louis Brandeis, found the precedent he established in *Schenck* returned to haunt him.

Defendants Jacob Abrams and four colleagues, all Russian immigrants, were charged with violating the Espionage Act and the 1918 Sedition Amendment. They had printed two leaflets criticizing

United States involvement in Russian affairs, specifically, the dispatch of American troops to Russia allegedly to put down the communist revolution. The second pamphlet was printed in Yiddish and called for a general strike. Some of the subversive material was secretly distributed throughout New York. Others were simply scattered by dropping them from the window of a building where one of the defendants worked.

Writing for the Court majority, Justice John H. Clark found his authority to dismiss the defendants' First Amendment claims in Holmes's earlier efforts.

> On the record thus described it is argued, somewhat faintly, that the acts charged against the defendants were not unlawful because [they were] within the protection of that freedom of speech and of the press which is guaranteed by the First Amendment to the Constitution of the United States, and that the entire Espionage Act is unconstitutional because [it is] in conflict with that Amendment.
>
> This contention is sufficiently discussed and is definitely negatived in *Schenck v. United States* and *Baer v. United States*, 249 U.S. 47; and in *Frohwerk v. United States*, 249 U.S. 204.[21]

Holmes attempted to clarify his clear and present danger test explaining that "it is only the present danger of immediate evil or an intent to bring it about that warrants Congress in setting a limit to the expression of opinion where private rights are not concerned. Congress certainly cannot forbid all effort to change the mind of the country."[22]

It was, however, at least for the moment, too late. The cat was out of the bag, let loose in *Schenck*.

"Now nobody can suppose," Holmes wrote, "that the surreptitious publishing of a silly leaflet by an unknown man, without more, would present any immediate danger that its opinions would hinder the success of the government arms or have any appreciable tendency to do so."[23]

Having disposed of the constitutionality of the issue in *Schenck* the 7–2 majority felt no need to consider Holmes's current excursion into the meaning and intended application of the First Amendment. The question considered by seven of the nine justices was not a First

Amendment issue, but whether there was "substantial evidence in the record to support the judgment upon the verdict of guilty" at the trial.[24] The justices believed there was.

Holmes and Brandeis did not. Now, eight months after *Schenck*, Holmes began to consider and to discuss the First Amendment implications of the congressional legislation. In the dissent that has led many to see Holmes as a champion of free speech and the First Amendment, the jurist concluded with a powerful discourse.

> Prosecution for the expression of opinions seems to me perfectly logical. If you have no doubt of your premises or your power and want a certain result with all your heart you naturally express your wishes in law and sweep away all opposition. To allow opposition by speech seems to indicate that you think the speech impotent, as when a man says that he has squared the circle, or that you do not care whole-heartedly for the result, or that you doubt either your power or your premises. But when men have realized that time has upset many fighting faiths, they may come to believe even more than they believe the very foundations of their own conduct that the ultimate good desired is better reached in the free trade of ideas—that the best test of truth is the power of the thought to get itself accepted in the competition of the market, and that truth is the only ground upon which their wishes safely can be carried out. That at any rate is the theory of our Constitution. It is an experiment, as all life is an experiment. Every year if not every day we have to wager our salvation upon some prophecy based upon imperfect knowledge. While that experiment is part of our system I think that we should be externally vigilant against attempts to check the expression of opinions that we loathe and believe to be fraught with death, unless they so imminently threaten immediate interference with the lawful and pressing purposes of the law that an immediate check is required to save the country. I wholly disagree with the argument of the Government that the First Amendment left the common law as to seditious libel in force. History seems to me against the notion. I had conceived that the United States through many years had shown its repentance for the Sedition Act of 1798, by repaying fines that it imposed. Only the emergency that makes it immediately dangerous to

leave the correction of evil councils to time warrants making any exception to the sweeping command, "Congress shall make no law . . . abridging the freedom of speech." Of course I am speaking only of expressions of opinion and exhortations, which were all that were uttered here, but I regret that I cannot put into more impressive words my belief in their conviction upon this indictment the defendants were deprived of their rights under the Constitution of the United States.[25]

Now, in the process of considering the specific actions of Abrams and his codefendants, Holmes espoused a level of protection he believed the Constitution offered. Unlike his *Schenck* opinion, Holmes talked about the Constitution, its meaning and its application. Yet Holmes's clear and present danger test was never used by the majority in a manner that benefited defendants accused of sedition against the United States. The *Abrams* majority in effect rejected Holmes's intended meaning of clear and present danger and substituted for the notion of immediate evils, the mere "tendency" of speech to cause illegal actions. Even as Holmes attempted to refine the clear and present danger test and to bring it in line with his now considered beliefs about the First Amendment, others on the Court retreated to a more repressive standard.

Reflections

Schenck v. United States did not provide a thoughtful analysis of the First Amendment, but it did introduce the Supreme Court to the tentative first steps of First Amendment theory within the context of judicial deliberations and the complex intricacies of the American legal system. The role of First Amendment theory in jurisprudence has grown significantly since 1919. Chief Justice Charles Evans Hughes wrote in 1937:

> The greater the importance of safeguarding the community from incitements to the overthrow of our institutions by force and violence, the more imperative is the need to preserve inviolate the constitutional rights of free speech, free press and free assembly in order to maintain the opportunity for free political discussion, to the end that gov-

ernment may be responsive to the will of the people and that changes, if desired, may be obtained by peaceful means. Therein lies the security of the Republic, the very foundation of constitutional government.[26]

On January 23, 1920, *Schenck* coprosecutor Alfred Bettman testified before the Rules Committee of the House of Representatives. He did not mention specifically his role in the Schenck prosecution, but he warned the committee against the dangers of vague language in sedition legislation. "[Statutory] language which penalizes not what a man actually did," Bettman said, "but the tendency of what he may have said, or the tendency of what he may have written, is the kind of thing which was . . . repudiated by the states when the first amendment was put in the Constitution."[27]

Bettman told the House Committee he saw no need for new sedition legislation. "The lesson that we have had since the war," Bettman said, "is that the emotions and passions that are engendered by the enforcement of [sedition laws], unfortunately cannot be immediately cut off, but continue."[28] Bettman's co-counsel in the *Schenck* prosecution, John Lord O'Brian, took a similar stance thirty-two years later in an article in the *Harvard Law Review*. O'Brian warned of the "numerous occasions since the First World War, and increasingly since the Second World War, on which the power of the courts has been invoked to limit as well as to protect the liberties of the citizen under the First Amendment."[29]

"Freedom of thought," the former prosecutor explained, "freedom to express opinions, and in particular freedom to criticize are the phrases most important to us, because they provide the warp and woof of our democratic social structure."[30]

The threat to democracy raised by state and private abridgments of free expression is always present. Forty-six laws relating to espionage and sabotage were passed by Congress between 1917 and 1976.[31] The Smith Act remains on the books. Individual decisions by the judiciary have in some cases reduced the danger of government interference with speech. Yet problems continue to surface as the nation celebrates two hundred years of constitutional law. In 1987 the Supreme Court upheld a government decision to require the National Film Board of Canada to clearly label as "propaganda" three films on acid rain before showing them in the United States. The labeling does not violate the First Amendment, the Court said.[32] Under sections of the federal immigration code, writer Margaret Randall, a teacher at the University of New Mexico, was denied repatriation status. Among the evidence weighed at her hearing was an article she had written concluding that Cuban women were, generally, better off since Castro's revolution.[33] A Columbian writer attempting to enter the United States on an invitation from Columbia University in New York to be part of a journalism awards ceremony also found herself in trouble with immigration officials. Patricia Lara was identified by officers at Kennedy Airport as someone on their official "lookout list." Her leftist writings made her visit inappropriate and after several days of questioning and detention, she too was deported.[34]

Congressional hearings were held during the summer of 1987 — the two hundredth anniversary of the Constitution. They exposed secret United States arms sales to Iran, profits from which were used to get around a congressional ban on military aid to Nicaraguan rebels attempting to overthrow their government. Broadcast live on television and radio, the hearings exemplified the constitutional role of the marketplace of ideas, the rejection of seditious libel as a crime, and justification for the founders' fear of government secrecy. Yet just months earlier, a major player in the episode warned the press to tread lightly when it came to disclosing information about the government. William Casey, appointed by President Ronald Reagan to run the Central Intelligence Agency, told a gathering of media lawyers that the right to publish was not absolute. Casey reminded the audience that the government already possessed numerous statutes making it a crime to publish information classified as secret. The director of intelligence then told his listeners that national interests would be served best by a new criminal statute that would make it possible to call the press to task for further unauthorized disclosures.[35]

Governmental abuses of the freedom to speak and of its corollary, the citizen's right to listen, are less frequent now than they were sixty years ago. They are less frequent than they were thirty-five years ago during the heat of the cold war. Yet the occasional attempts by government to shelter its citizens from subversive, seditious or simply controversial speech continues. Demonstrators attempting to exercise their First Amendment right to peaceful assembly too often find themselves the object of government harassment, bullying and arrest.

Much of our sense of what the First Amendment means, of the limits it places on government, and of its role in our democracy, traces its roots to *Schenck v. United States*. We accept *Schenck* as First Amendment precedent and we have built a judicial and philosophical structure upon the *Schenck* foundation. *Schenck* is a weak foundation—both philosophically and juristically. The history of the notion of "clear and present danger" as a safeguard for democracy is a history at odds with the founders' willingness to accept the risks inherent in a government based on a truly open marketplace of ideas. The use of *Schenck* as a foundation for the belief that the First Amendment is not absolute in the arena of public speech is misguided. Based on close examination of the judicial process, it is a notion to be revised or abandoned.[36]

In the final analysis, however, the ultimate safeguard of the right to speak freely may not lie with the courts, but with the vigilance of the individual citizen who understands the value of free expression and the complex application of the First Amendment in the American judicial process.

Espionage Act of June 15, 1917

Chap. 30.—An Act to punish acts of interference with the foreign relations, the neutrality, and the foreign commerce of the United States, to punish espionage, and better to enforce the criminal laws of the United States, and for other purposes.

"Be it enacted by the Senate and House of Representatives of the United States of America in Congress assembled:

TITLE I

ESPIONAGE

Section 1. That (a) whoever, for the purpose of obtaining information respecting the national defense with intent or reason to believe that the information to be obtained is to be used to the injury of the United States, or to the advantage of any foreign nation, goes upon, enters, flies over, or otherwise obtains information concerning any vessel, aircraft, work of defense, navy yard, naval station, submarine base, coaling station, fort, battery, torpedo station, dockyard, canal, railroad, arsenal, camp, factory, mine, telegraph, telephone, wireless or signal station, building, office, or other place connected with the national defense, owned or constructed, or in progress of construction by the United States or under the control of the United States, or of any of its officers or agents, or within the exclusive jurisdiction of the United States, or any place in which any vessel, aircraft, arms, munitions, or other materials or instruments for use in time of war are being made, prepared, repaired, or stored, under any contract or agreement with the United States, or with any person on behalf of the United States, or otherwise on behalf of the United States, or any prohibited place within the meaning of section six of this title; or (b) whoever for the purpose aforesaid, and with like intent or reason to believe, copies, takes, makes, or obtains, or attempts, or induces or aids another to copy, take, make, or obtain, any sketch, photograph, photographic negative, blue print, plan, map, model, instrument, appliance, document, writing, or note of anything connected with the national defense; or (c) whoever, for the purpose aforesaid, receives or obtains or agrees or attempts or induces or aids another to receive or obtain from any person, or from any source whatever, any document, writing, code book, signal book, sketch, photograph, photographic negative, blue print, plan, map, model, instrument, appliance, or note, of anything connected with the national defense, knowing or having reason to believe, at the time he receives or obtains, or agrees or attempts or induces or aids another to receive or obtain it, that it has been or will be obtained, taken, made or disposed of by any person contrary to the provisions of this title; or (d) whoever, lawfully or unlawfully having possession of, access to, control over, or being intrusted with any document, writing, code book, signal book, sketch, photograph, photographic negative, blue print, plan, map, model, instrument, appliance, or note relating to the national defense, willfully communicates or transmits or attempts to communicate or transmit the same to any person not entitled to receive it, or willfully retains the same and fails to deliver it on demand to the officer or employee of the United States entitled to receive it; or (e) whoever, being intrusted with or having lawful possession or control of any document, writing, code book, signal book, sketch, photograph, photographic negative, blue print, plan, map, model, note, or information, relating to the national defense, through gross negligence permits the same to be removed from its proper place of custody or delivered to anyone in violation of his trust, or to be lost, stolen, abstracted, or destroyed, shall be punished by a fine of not more than $10,000, or by imprisonment for not more than two years, or both.

Sec. 2. (a) Whoever, with intent or reason to believe that it is to be used to the injury of the United States or to the advantage of a foreign nation, communicates, delivers, or transmits, or attempts to, or aids or induces another to, communicate, deliver, or transmit, to any foreign government, or to any faction or party or military or naval force within a foreign country, whether recognized or unrecognized by the United States, or to any representative, officer, agent, employee, subject, or citizen thereof, either directly or indirectly, any document, writing, code book, signal book, sketch, photograph, photographic negative, blue print, plan, map, model, note, instrument, appliance, or information relating to the national defense, shall be punished by imprisonment for not more than twenty years: **Provided,** That whoever shall violate the provisions of subsection (a) of this section in time of war shall be punished by death or imprisonment for not more than thirty years; and (b) whoever, in time of war, with intent that the same shall be communicated to the enemy, shall collect, record, publish, or communicate, or attempt to elicit any information with respect to the movement, numbers, description, condition, or disposition of any of the armed forces, ships, aircraft, or war materials of the United States, or with respect to the plans or conduct, or supposed plans or conduct of any naval or military operations, or with respect to any works or measures undertaken for or connected with, or intended for the fortification or defense of any place, or any other information relating to the public defense, which might be useful to the enemy, shall be punished by death or by imprisonment for not more than thirty years.

Sec. 3. Whoever, when the United States is at war, shall willfully make or convey false reports or false statements with intent to interfere with the operation or success of the military or naval forces of the United States or to promote the success of its enemies and whoever, when the United States is at war, shall willfully cause or attempt to cause insubordination, disloyalty, mutiny, or refusal of duty, in the military or naval forces of the United States, or shall willfully obstruct the recruiting or enlistment service of the United States, to the injury of the service or of the United States, shall be punished by a fine of not more than $10,000 or imprisonment for not more than twenty years, or both.

Sec. 4. If two or more persons conspire to violate the provisions of sections two or three of this title, and one or more of such persons does any act to effect the object of the conspiracy, each of the parties to such conspiracy shall be punished as in said sections provided in the case of the doing of the act the accomplishment of which is the object of such conspiracy. Except as above provided conspiracies to commit offenses under this title shall be punished as provided by section thirty-seven of the Act to codify, revise, and amend the penal laws of the United States approved March fourth, nineteen hundred and nine.

Sec. 5. Whoever harbors or conceals any person who he knows, or has reasonable grounds to believe or suspect, has committed, or is about to commit, an offense under this title shall be punished by a fine of not more than $10,000 or by imprisonment for not more than two years, or both.

Sec. 6. The President in time of war or in case of national emergency may by proclamation designate any place other than those set forth in subsection (a) of section one hereof in which anything for the use of the Army or Navy is being prepared or constructed or stored as a prohibited place for the purposes of this title: **Provided,** That he shall determine that information with respect thereto would be prejudicial to the national defense.

Sec. 7. Nothing contained in this title shall be deemed to limit the jurisdiction of the general courts-martial, military commissions, or naval courts-martial under sections thirteen hundred and forty-two, thirteen hundred and forty-three, and sixteen hundred and twenty-four of the Revised Statutes as amended.

Sec. 8. The provisions of this title shall extend to all Territories, possessions, and places subject to the jurisdiction of the United States whether or not contiguous thereto, and offenses under this title when committed upon the high seas or elsewhere within the admiralty and maritime jurisdiction of the United States and outside the territorial limits thereof shall be punishable hereunder.

Sec. 9. The Act entitled "An Act to prevent the disclosure of national defense secrets," approved March third, nineteen hundred and eleven, is hereby repealed.

Amendment of May 16, 1918, to Section 3 of the Espionage Act

Chap. 75.—An Act to amend section three, title one, of the Act entitled "An Act to punish acts of interference with the foreign relations, the neutrality, and the foreign commerce of the United States, to punish espionage, and better to enforce the criminal laws of the United States, and for other purposes," approved June fifteenth, nineteen hundred and seventeen, and for other purposes. Be it enacted by the Senate and House of Representatives of the United States of America in Congress assembled, That section three of title one of the Act entitled "An Act to punish acts of interference with the foreign relations, the neutrality, and the foreign commerce of the United States, to punish espionage, and better to enforce the criminal laws of the United States, and for other purposes," approved June fifteenth, nineteen hundred and seventeen, be, and the same is hereby, amended so as to read as follows:

"**Sec. 3.** Whoever, when the United States is at war, shall willfully make or convey false reports or false statements with intent to interfere with the operation or success of the military or naval forces of the United States, or to promote the success of its enemies, or shall willfully make or convey false reports or false statements, or say or do anything except by way of bona fide and not disloyal advice to an investor or investors, with intent to obstruct the sale by the United States of bonds or other securities of the United States or the making of loans by or to the United States, and whoever, when the United

States is at war, shall willfully cause or attempt to cause, or incite or
attempt to incite, insubordination, disloyalty, mutiny, or refusal of
duty, in the military or naval forces of the United States, or shall
willfully obstruct or attempt to obstruct the recruiting or enlistment
service of the United States, and whoever, when the United States is
at war, shall willfully utter, print, write, or publish any disloyal, pro-
fane, scurrilous, or abusive language about the form of government
of the United States, or the Constitution of the United States, or the
military or naval forces of the United States, or the flag of the United
States, or the uniform of the Army or Navy of the United States, or
any language intended to bring the form of government of the United
States, or the Constitution of the United States, or the military or
naval forces of the United States, or the flag of the United States, or
the uniform of the Army or Navy of the United States into contempt,
scorn, contumely, or disrepute, or shall willfully utter, print, write, or
publish any language intended to incite, provoke, or encourage resist-
ance to the United States, or to promote the cause of its enemies, or
shall willfully display the flag of any foreign enemy, or shall willfully
by utterance, writing, printing, publication, or language spoken,
urge, incite, or advocate any curtailment of production in this country of any thing or things, product or products, necessary or essential
to the prosecution of the war in which the United States may be
engaged, with intent by such curtailment to cripple or hinder the
United States in the prosecution of the war, and whoever shall willfully advocate, teach, defend, or suggest the doing of any of the acts
or things in this section enumerated, and whoever shall by word or
act support or favor the cause of any country with which the United
States is at war or by word or act oppose the cause of the United
States therein, shall be punished by a fine of not more than $10,000
or imprisonment for not more than twenty years, or both: **Provided,**
That any employee or official of the United States Government who
commits any disloyal act or utters any unpatriotic or disloyal language, or who, in an abusive and violent manner criticizes the Army
or Navy or the flag of the United States shall be at once dismissed
from the service. Any such employee shall be dismissed by the head of
the department in which the employee may be engaged, and any
such official shall be dismissed by the authority having power to
appoint a successor to the dismissed official."

Sec. 2. That section one of Title XII and all other provisions of the Act entitled "An Act to punish acts of interference with the foreign relations, the neutrality, and the foreign commerce of the United States, to punish espionage, and better to enforce the criminal laws of the United States, and for other purposes," approved June fifteenth, nineteen hundred and seventeen, which apply to section three to Title I thereof shall apply with equal force and effect to said section three as amended.

Title XII of the said Act of June fifteenth, nineteen hundred and seventeen, be, and the same is hereby, amended by adding thereto the following section:

Sec. 4. When the United States is at war, the Postmaster General may, upon evidence satisfactory to him that any person or concern is using the mails in violation of any of the provisions of this Act, instruct the postmaster at any post office at which mail is received addressed to such person or concern to return to the postmaster at the office at which they were originally mailed all letters or other matter so addressed, with the words 'Mail to this address undeliverable under Espionage Act' plainly written or stamped upon the outside thereof, and all such letters or other matters so returned to such postmasters shall be by them returned to the senders thereof under such relations as the Postmaster General may prescribe."

Approved, May 16, 1918.

Schenck v. United States

Mr. Justice Holmes delivered the opinion of the court.

This is an indictment in three counts. The first charges a conspiracy to violate the Espionage Act of June 15, 1917, c.30, § 3, 40 Stat. 217, 219, by causing and attempting to cause insubordination, &c., in the military and naval forces of the United States, and to obstruct the recruiting and enlistment service of the United States, when the United States was at war with the German Empire, to wit, that the defendants wilfully conspired to have printed and circulated to men who had been called and accepted for military service under the Act of May 18, 1917, a document set forth and alleged to be calculated to men who had been called and accepted for military service under the Act of May 18, 1917, a document set forth and alleged to be calculated to cause such insubordination and obstruction. The count alleges overt acts in pursuance of the conspiracy, ending in the distribution of the document set forth. The second count alleges a conspiracy to commit an offence against the United States, to wit, to use the mails for the transmission of matter declared to be non-mailable by Title XII, § 2 of the Act of June 15, 1917, to wit, the above mentioned document, with an averment of the same overt acts. The third count charges an unlawful use of the mails for the transmission of the same matter and otherwise as above. The defendants were found guilty on all the counts. They set up the First Amendment to the Constitution forbidding Congress to make any law abridging the freedom of speech, or of the press, and bringing the case here on that ground have argued some other points also of which we must dispose.

It is argued that the evidence, if admissible, was not sufficient to prove that the defendant Schenck was concerned in sending the documents. According to the testimony Schenck said he was general secretary of the Socialist party and had charge of the Socialist headquarters from which the documents were sent. He identified a book found there as the minutes of the Executive Committee of the party. The book showed a resolution of August 13, 1917, that 15,000 leaflets should be printed on the other side of one of them in use, to be mailed to men who had passed exemption boards, and for distribution. Schenck personally attended to the printing. On August 20 the general secretary's report said "Obtained new leaflets from printer and started work addressing envelopes" &c.; and there was a resolve that Comrade Schenck be allowed $125 for sending leaflets through the mail. He said that he had about fifteen or sixteen thousand printed. There were files of the circular in question in the inner office which he said were printed on the other side of the one-sided circular and were there for distribution. Other copies were proved to have been sent through the mails to drafted men. Without going into confirmatory details that were proved, no reasonable man could doubt that the defendant Schenck was largely instrumental in sending the circulars about. As to the defendant Baer there was evidence that she was a member of the Executive Board and that the minutes of its transactions were hers. The argument as to the sufficiency of the evidence that the defendants conspired to send the documents only impairs the seriousness of the real defence.

It is objected that the documentary evidence was not admissible because obtained upon a search warrant, valid so far as appears. The contrary is established. Adams v. New York, 192 U.S. 585; Weeks v. United States, 232 U.S. 383, 395, 396. The search warrant did not issue against the defendant but against the socialist headquarters at 1326 Arch Street and it would seem that the documents technically were not even in the defendants' possession. See Johnson v. United States, 228 U.S. 457. Notwithstanding some protest in argument the notion that evidence even directly proceeding from the defendant in a criminal proceeding is excluded in all cases by the Fifth Amendment is plainly unsound. Holt v. United States, 218 U.S. 245, 252, 253.

The document in question upon its first printed side recited the first section of the Thirteenth amendment, said that the idea embodied in it was violated by the Conscription Act and that a conscript is little better than a convict. In impassioned language it intimated that conscription was despotism in its worst form and a monstrous wrong against humanity in the interest of Wall Street's chosen few. It said "Do not submit to intimidation," but in form at least confined itself to peaceful measure such as a petition for the repeal of the act. The other and later printed side of the sheet was headed "Assert Your Rights." It stated reasons for alleging that any one violated the Constitution when he refused to recognize "your right to assert your opposition to the draft," and went on "If you do not assert and support your rights, you are helping to deny or disparage rights which it is the solemn duty of all citizens and residents of the United States to retain." It described the arguments on the other side as coming from cunning politicians and a mercenary capitalist press, and even silent consent to the conscription law as helping to support an infamous conspiracy. It denied the power to send our citizens away to foreign shores to shoot up the people of other lands, and added that words could not express the condemnation such cold-blooded ruthlessness deserves, &c., 7c., winding up "You must do your share to maintain, support and uphold the rights of the people of this country." Of course the document would not have been sent unless it had been intended to have some effect, and we do not see what effect it could be expected to have upon persons subject to the draft except to influence them to obstruct the carrying of it out. The defendants do not deny that the jury might find against them on this point.

But it is said, suppose that that was the tendency of this circular, it is protected by the First Amendment to the Constitution. Two of the strongest expressions are said to be quoted respectively from well-known public men. It well may be that the prohibition of laws abridging the freedom of speech is not confined to previous restraints, although to prevent them may have been the main purpose, as intimated in Patterson v. Colorado, 205 U.S. 454, 462. We admit that in many places and in ordinary times the defendants in saying all that was said in the circular would have been within their constitutional rights. But the character of every act depends upon the circumstances in which it is done. Aikens v. Wisconsin, 195 U.S. 194, 205, 206. The most stringent protection of free speech would not protect a man in falsely shouting fire in a theatre and causing a panic. It does not even protect a man from an injunction against uttering words that may have all the effect of force. Gompers v. Bucks Stove & Range

Co., 221 U.S. 418, 439. The question in every case is whether the words used are used in such circumstances and are of such a nature as to create a clear and present danger that they will bring about the substantive evils that Congress has a right to prevent. It is a question of proximity and degree. When a nation is at war many things that might be said in time of peace are such a hindrance to its effort that their utterance will not be endured so long as men fight and that no Court could regard them as protected by any constitutional right. It seems to be admitted that if an actual obstruction of the recruiting service were proved, liability for words that produced that effect might be enforced. The statute of 1917 in § 4 punishes conspiracies to obstruct as well as actual obstruction. If the act (speaking, or circulating a paper), its tendency and the intent with which it is done are the same, we perceive no ground for saying that success alone warrants making the act a crime. Goldman v. United States, 245 U.S. 474, 477. Indeed that case might be said to dispose of the present contention if the precedent covers all media concludendi. But as the right to free speech was not referred to specially, we have thought fit to add a few words.

It was not argued that a conspiracy to obstruct the draft was not within the words of the Act of 1917. The words are "obstruct the recruiting or enlistment service," and it might be suggested that they refer only to making it hard to get volunteers. Recruiting heretofore usually having been accomplished by getting volunteers the word is apt to call up that method only in our minds. But recruiting is gaining fresh supplies for the forces, as well by draft as otherwise. It is put as an alternative to enlistment or voluntary enrollment in this act. The fact that the Act of 1917 was enlarged by the amending Act of May 16, 1918, c.75, 40 Stat. 553, of course, does not affect the present indictment and would not, even if the former act had been repealed. Rev. Stats., § 13.

Judgments affirmed.

Notes

CHAPTER 1

1. For a general history of newspapers and freedom of expression in the United States, see Edwin Emery and Michael Emery, *The Press and America, An Interpretive History of the Mass Media*, 5th ed. (Englewood Cliffs, New Jersey: Prentice Hall, 1984).

2. *Schenck v. United States* 249 U.S. 47 (1919).

3. Professor Don Pember writes, "There is a debate within the legal-historical community over the meaning of the First Amendment when it was drafted and approved in the late eighteenth century. Some persons argue that it was intended to block both prior censorship and prosecution for seditious libel. Others argue that it prohibits only prior censorship. We will probably never know what the guarantee of freedom of expression meant to the persons who drafted it, but it is a good bet that citizens had a wide variety of interpretations of the First Amendment when they voted to approve it." Don R. Pember, *Mass Media Law*, 4th ed. (Dubuque, Iowa: William C. Brown, 1987), p. 53; The two schools of thought on this issue are well represented by Leonard W. Levy, *Emergence of a Free Press* (New York: Oxford Press, 1985) and Jeffrey Smith, *Printers and Press Freedom* (New York: Oxford Press, 1987).

4. "Marshall Sounds Critical Note on Bicentennial," *New York Times*, 7 May 1987.

5. William Rehnquist, "The Notion of a Living Constitution," in *Views From the Bench*, ed. Mark Cannon and David O'Brian (Chatham, New Jersey: Chatham House Pub., 1985), p. 128.

6. Alexander Hamilton, No.84: *The Federalist Papers*.

CHAPTER 2

1. See *Schenck v. United States,* 249 U.S. 47 (1919); *Frohwerk v. United States,* 249 U.S. 204 (1919); *Debs v. United States,* 249 U.S. 211 (1919); *Abrams v. United States,* 250 U.S. 616 (1919).

2. Espionage Act of 15 June 1917, 40 Stat. 217.

3. Espionage Act, 40 Stat. 553 (amended 1918).

4. Van Vechten Veeder, "History of the Law of Defamation," in *Select Essays in Anglo-American Legal History*, ed. and comp. Committee of the Association of American Law Schools, 3 vols. (Boston, 1909), 3:453–4. Useful histories of sedition in the United States include: Zechariah Chafee, Jr., *Free Speech in the United States* (Cambridge,

Mass.: Harvard Univ. Press, 1941); Leonard Levy, *Emergence of a Free Press* (New York: Oxford Univ. Press, 1985); John Miller, *Crisis in Freedom* (Boston: Little Brown & Co., 1951). Sedition in England is covered in Fredrick Siebert, *Freedom of the Press in England 1476-1776* (Urbana: Univ. of Illinois Press, 1965).

5. *Rex v. Twyn*, in Howell, *State Trials*, 6:513, 536 (1663).

6. Levy, *Emergence of a Free Press*, p.16.

7. Ibid.

8. John Roche, "American Liberty: An Examination of the Tradition of Freedom," in *Shadow and Substance, Essays on the Theory and Structure of Politics* (London: Collier Books, 1964).

9. First Amendment scholar Don Pember suggests that in 1790 the First Amendment's "guarantee of freedom of expression meant different things to different people. In fact, one can speculate that the inherent vagueness in the constitutional guarantee enhanced its chances of being adopted." Don Pember, *Mass Media Law*, 4th ed. (Dubuque, Iowa: William C. Brown, 1987), p.49.

10. Emery and Emery, *The Press and America*, pp.100-105.

11. *See generally* Margaret Blanchard, "Filling the Void: Speech and Press in State Courts Prior to *Gitlow*," *The First Amendment Reconsidered*, ed. Bill Chamberlain and Charlene Brown (New York: Longman, 1982).

12. Thomas Cooley, *A Treatise on the Constitutional Limitations Which Rest Upon the Legislative Power of the States of the American Union*, 2d ed. (Boston: Little Brown & Co., 1871), p. 513.

13. Timothy Gleason, "Legal Practice and Freedom of the Press: An Introduction to an Unfamiliar Terrain," *Journalism History*, vol. 14, no. 1 (Spring 1987): 26, at p. 27.

14. "The Soap-Box Preachers of Sedition," *New York Times*, 16 Sept. 1917, Editorial section.

15. "Pacifists Arrested in Stormy Meeting," *New York Times*, 17 Sept. 1917, p.4.

16. "Mrs. Hale is Released," *New York Times*, 20 Sept. 1917, p.8.

17. "Columbia is Closed to Pacifist Junior," *New York Times*, 18 Sept. 1917, p.9.

18. "Ban on Scott Nearing," *New York Times*, 19 Sept. 1917.

19. "Patriots and Traitors," *New York Times*, 17 Sept. 1917, Editorial section.

20. *See generally* Zechariah Chafee, *Free Speech in the United States;* Blair Coan, *The Red Web*, American Classics Edition (Boston: Western Islands, 1969); Henry Steel Commanger, *The American Mind* (New Haven: Yale Univ. Press, 1966); John Lofton, *The Press as Guardian of the First Amendment* (Columbia: Univ. of South Carolina Press, 1980); Paul Murphy, *The Meaning of Freedom of Speech: First Amendment Freedoms from Wilson to FDR* (Westport, Conn.: Greenwood Pub. Co., 1972); William Preston, *Aliens and Dissenters: Federal Suppression of Radicals 1903-1933* (Cambridge: Harvard Univ. Press, 1963); John Roche, *The Quest for the Dream* (Chicago: Quadrangle Books, 1968); Ronald Steele, *Walter Lippmann and the American Century* (Boston: Little Brown & Co., 1980).

21. "100 Radical Papers May Be Suppressed," *New York Times*, 16 Sept. 1917, p.7.

22. "Liberty's Editor Arrested," *New York Times*, 16 Sept. 1917, p. 7.

23. "Puts Tougher Rein on 'Language' Press," *New York Times,* 20 Sept. 1917, p.6.

24. David Bogen, "The Free Speech Metamorphosis of Mr. Justice Holmes," *Hofstra Law Review* 11 (Fall 1982):97-189; Robert Cover, "The Left, The Right and the First Amendment: 1918-1928," *Maryland Law Review* 40 (1981):349-391; Gerald Gunther, "Learned Hand and the Origins of Modern First Amendment Doctrine: Some Fragments of History," *Stanford Law Review* 27 (February 1975):719-72; Hans Linde, " 'Clear and Present Danger' Reexamined: Dissonance in the Brandenberg Concerto," *Stanford Law Review* 22 (June 1970):1163-86; David Rabban, "The First Amendment in its Forgotten Years," *Yale Law Journal* 90 (January 1981):514-95; Fred Ragan, "Justice Oliver Wendell Holmes, Jr., Zechariah Chafee, Jr., and the Clear and Present Danger Test for Free Speech: The First Year: 1919," *The Journal of American History* 58 (June 1971):24-45; Yosal Rogat and James O'Fallon, "Mr. Justice Holmes: A Dissenting Opinion—The Speech Cases," *Stanford Law Review* 36 (July 1984):1349-1406; Frank Strong, "Fifty Years of 'Clear and Present Danger,' " in *The Supreme Court Review, 1969,* ed. Philip Kurland (Chicago: Univ. of Chicago Press, 1969) pp. 41-80.

25. *Scales v. United States,* 367 U.S. 203 (1961). *See also Yates v. United States,* 354 U.S. 298 (1957).

26. *Brandenburg v. Ohio,* 395 U.S. 444 (1969)

27. *Brandenburg v. Ohio,* 395 U.S. 444, at 447.

28. *New York Times Co. v. United States; United States v. Washington Post,* 713 U.S. 403 (1971).

29. Zechariah Chafee, "Freedom of Speech in War Time," *Harvard Law Review* 32 (1919):932-973, 967.

30. The repression of minority-owned newspapers is discussed in Patrick Washburn, *A Matter of Sedition* (New York: Oxford Univ. Press, 1986).

31. *See* Anthony Lewis, "U.S. Treatment of Journalist an Embarrassment to Americans," *Los Angeles Daily Journal,* 3 Dec. 1986, p. 4.

32. *Schenck v. United States,* 249 U.S. 47, 51 (1919).

33. Frank Snepp, *Decent Interval* (New York: Random House, 1977).

34. *Snepp v. United States,* 5 Med. L. Rptr. 2409, 2411 (1980).

35. *See* note 1, Chapter 1. A useful discussion is found in Franklyn Haiman, *Speech and Law in a Free Society* (Chicago: Univ. of Chicago Press, 1981).

36. Alexander Meiklejohn, *Political Freedom* (New York: Oxford Univ. Press, A Galaxy Book, 1965), p.30.

37. Linde, " 'Clear and Present Danger' Reexamined," p. 1163.

38. Quoted in Alexander Bickel, *The Supreme Court and the Idea of Progress* (New Haven: Yale Univ. Press, 1978), p. 27. Debs, like Schenck, was prosecuted under the Espionage Act and convicted. Holmes wrote the *Debs* opinion for a unanimous Court. *See Debs v. United States,* 249 U.S. 211 (1919).

39. Henry Black, *Black's Law Dictionary,* 5th ed. (St. Paul, Minn.: West Pub. Co., 1979), p. 767.

CHAPTER 3

1. *New York Times,* 9 Jan. 1919, p. 18.

2. *New York Times,* 9 Jan. 1919, p.1.

3. The Supreme Court overturned Berger's conviction under the Espionage Act in *Berger v. United States,* 252 U.S. 22 (1921) on the grounds that the trial judge had shown prejudice. *See generally* Lofton, *The Press as Guardian.*

4. Henry J. Gibbons and Henry John Nelson, "Brief of Plaintiffs-in-Error," *Landmark Briefs and Arguments of the Supreme Court of the United States: Constitutional Law,* vol. 18 (Arlington, Va.: Univ. Pub. of America, 1975), p. 996.

5. *New York Times,* 9 Jan. 1919, p. 2.

6. Ibid.

7. Ironically, O'Brian wrote an article in 1952 entitled "New Encroachments on Individual Freedom," *Harvard Law Review* 66 (November 1952):1-27. O'Brian in fact wrote Zechariah Chafee to contradict the Harvard law professor's 1917 attacks on the vitality of Justice Department enforcement of the Espionage Act. Chafee biographer Donald Smith wrote that O'Brian was offended by Chafee's suggestion that the act was used as a dragnet for pacifists. O'Brian, Smith says, claimed the Justice Department attempted to hold down the number of prosecutions "despite strong community pressures to prosecute." Donald Smith, *Zechariah Chafee, Jr. Defender of Liberty and Law* (Cambridge, Mass.: Harvard Univ. Press, 1986), pp.38-40.

8. Selective Draft Act of May 18, 1917.

9. *Arver v. United States,* 245 U.S. 366 (1918).

10. John Lord O'Brian and Alfred Bettman, "Brief for the United States," *Landmark Briefs,* p. 1027.

11. Ibid., p. 1028.

12. Ibid., p. 1027.

13. Ibid.

14. Ibid., p. 1032.

15. Ibid.

16. Ibid. p. 1028.

17. Ibid.

18. Ibid., pp. 1028-30.

19. Ibid., pp. 1030-32.

20. Ibid., p. 1032.

21. Oliver Wendell Holmes, *The Common Law* [1881], ed. Mark DeWolfe Howe (Boston: Little Brown & Co., 1963).

22. Holmes to Pollock, 24 November 1918, in Mark DeWolfe Howe, ed., *Holmes-Pollock Letters,* vol. 1 (Cambridge: Harvard Univ. Press, 1942), p. 274.

23. Elder Witt, ed., *The Supreme Court and its Work* (Washington, D.C.: Congressional Quarterly, 1981), p. 72. *See also* Leon Friedman and Fred L. Israel, eds., *The Justices of the United States Supreme Court 1789-1969,* vol. 3 (New York: R. R. Bowker Co., 1969); and G. Edward White, *The American Judicial Tradition* (New York: Oxford Univ. Press, 1976).

CHAPTER 4

1. The analysis of the defense and prosecution briefs in *Schenck* are based upon the attorneys' briefs. Transcripts of oral arguments before the Court were not made in 1919.

2. Gibbons and Nelson, "Brief of Plaintiffs-in-Error," p. 991. *See* Appendix A for Section 4, Title 1.

3. Ibid.

4. Ibid.

5. Ibid., pp. 991–92.

6. Ibid., p. 993

7. *Patterson v. Colorado*, 205 U.S. 454 (1907). S. Bogen has argued that Holmes's view in *Patterson*, that all prior restraints were unconstitutional, changed by the time Holmes wrote the *Schenck* decision. *See* Bogen, "The Free Speech Metamorphosis," pp. 144–50.

8. Gibbons and Nelson, "Brief of Plaintiffs-in-Error," p. 994.

9. Ibid., p. 995.

10. Ibid., p. 996.

11. Ibid.

12. The notion that prior restraints have always been frowned upon in the United States is no longer accepted without question. *See* John P. Roche, *Shadow and Substance*, pp. 3–38.

13. Gibbons and Nelson, "Brief of Plaintiffs-in-Error," p. 994.

14. Ibid., pp. 994–95.

15. Ibid., p. 997.

16. Ibid., p. 1002.

17. Ibid., pp. 1002–03.

18. Ibid., p. 1008.

19. Ibid.

20. Ibid.

21. Ibid., p. 1006.

22. Ibid., p. 1010.

23. Ibid., p. 1011.

24. Ibid.

25. Ibid.

26. Ibid., p. 1012.

27. Ibid., p. 1014.

28. Ibid., p. 1017.

29. *U.S. v. Tureaud*, 20 Fed. 621; *In the matter of a Rule of Court* 3 Woods 502; *exparte Bollman*, 4 Cranch 75, at 130; *U.S. v. Sapinkow*, 90 Fed. 6454, 660.

30. Gibbons and Nelson "Brief of Plaintiffs-in-Error," p. 1018.

31. Ibid., p. 1019.

32. O'Brian and Bettman, "Brief for the United States," p. 1037.

33. Ibid., pp. 1037–38.

34. Ibid., p. 1038.

35. Ibid.

36. Ibid., p. 1040.

37. *Ramp v. United States* was cited by the prosecution only as "Justice Department Bulletin 86."

38. O'Brian and Bettman, "Brief for the United States," p. 1044.

39. Ibid., p. 1043.

40. Ibid., p. 1043.

41. Ibid., pp. 1043–44.

42. Ibid., p. 1045.

43. Ibid., p. 1046.

44. Ibid., p. 1050.

45. Ibid.

46. Ibid., p. 1053.

47. Ibid., p. 1054.

48. Ibid.

49. Ibid., p. 1056.

50. Ibid., p. 1057.

51. Ibid., p. 1060.

52. There is no record to indicate the precise date the justices met in conference to discuss *Schenck*.

53. Holmes, *The Common Law*, p. 5.

54. Holmes, "The Path of the Law," p. 458.

CHAPTER 5

1. Friedman. *A History of American Law*, p. 13.

2. *Schenck v. United States*, 249 U.S. 47 (1919).

3. Abraham, *The Judicial Process*, 5th ed. (New York: Oxford Univ. Press, 1986), p. 369.

4. U.S. Constitution, Art. III, Sec. 1 and 2, read as follows:

SECTION 1. The judicial Power of the United States, shall be vested in one Supreme Court, and in such inferior Courts as the Congress may from time to time ordain and establish. The Judges, both of the supreme and inferior Courts, shall hold their Offices during good Behaviour, and shall, at stated Times, receive for their Services, a Compensation which shall not be diminished during their Continuance in Office.

SECTION 2. The judicial Power shall extend to all Cases, in Law and Equity, arising under this Constitution, the Laws of the United States, and Treaties made, or which shall be made, under their Authority; — to all Cases affecting Ambassadors, other public Ministers and Consuls; — to all Cases of admiralty and maritime Jurisdiction; — to Controversies to which the United States shall be a Party; — to Controversies between two or more States; — between a State and Citizens of another State; — between Citizens of different states; — between Citizens of the same State claiming Lands under Grants of different States, and between a State, or the Citizens thereof, and foreign States, Citizens or Subjects.

In all Cases affecting Ambassadors, other public Ministers and Consuls, and those in which a State shall be Party, the Supreme Court shall have original Jurisdiction. In all the other Cases before mentioned, the Supreme Court shall have appellate Jurisdiction, both as to Law and Fact, with such Exceptions, and under such Regulations as the Congress shall make.

The Trial of all Crimes, except in Cases of Impeachment, shall be by Jury; and such Trial shall be held in the State where the said Crimes shall have been committed; but when not committed within any State, the Trial shall be at such Place or Places as the Congress may by Law have directed.

5. *Marbury v. Madison,* 1 Cr. 137 (1803).

6. *See generally* John A. Garraty, "The Case of the Missing Commissions," in John A. Garraty, ed., *Quarrels That Have Shaped the Constitution* (New York: Harper and Row, 1962).

7. *See generally* Martin Shapiro, *Freedom of Speech: The Supreme Court and Judicial Review* (Englewood Cliffs,N.J.: Prentice-Hall, 1966); and Martin Shapiro, *Law and Politics in the Supreme Court* (New York: The Free Press, 1964).

8. Useful discussions of the political nature of Justice Marshall's handling of *Marbury v. Madison* are found in Archibald Cox, *The Court and the Constitution* (Boston: Houghton Mifflin Co., 1987); John Garraty, *The Case of the Missing Commissions.*

9. *Marbury v. Madison,* 1 Cr. 137, 176.

10. Abraham, *The Judicial Process,* p. 292.

11. *Marbury v. Madison,* 1 Cr. 137, 177.

12. United States, Constitution, Art. IV.

13. *Marbury v. Madison,* 1 Cr. 137, 177.

14. Ibid., p. 179.

15. Ibid., p. 180.

16. Archibald Cox, *The Role of the Supreme Court in American Government* (New York: Oxford Univ. Press, 1976).

17. *McCulloch v. Maryland,* 4 Wheat. 316 (1819).

18. *McCulloch v. Maryland,* 4 Wheat. 316, 400, 401.

19. Ibid., p. 407.

20. *Ogden v. Saunders,* 12 Wheat. 213 (1827).

21. Ibid.

22. *Barron v. Baltimore,* 7 Pet. 243 (1833).

23. *Barron v. Baltimore,* 7 Pet. 243, 249.

24. Ibid.

25. *Dred Scott v. Sanford,* 19 How. 393 (1857).

26. *See generally* Bruce Catton, "The Dred Scott Case," in *Quarrels That Have Shaped the Constitution,* ed. John A. Garraty (New York: Harper and Row, 1962).

27. *Stradder v. Graham,* 10 How. 82 (1850).

28. Catton, "The Dred Scott Case," p. 83.

29. C. Herman Pritchett, "Judicial Supremacy from Marshall to Berger," in

Essays on the Constitution of the United States, ed. M. Judd Harmon (Port Washington, N.Y.: Kennikat Press Corp., 1978), p. 202.

30. White, *The American Judicial Tradition,* p. 82.

31. Ibid.

32. Abraham, *The Judicial Process,* p. 376.

33. Arguments about the judicial role and the dangers of the appearance that the Court sometimes steps into the legislative arena are a consistently troublesome area for the Court. *See,* for example, Charles Beard, *The Supreme Court and the Constitution* [1912] (Englewood Cliffs, N.J.: Prentice-Hall, 1962); Raoul Berger, *Government by Judiciary* (Cambridge: Harvard Univ. Press, 1977); John Hart Ely, *Democracy and Distrust* (Cambridge: Harvard Univ. Press, 1980); and Blaine Free Moore, *The Supreme Court and Unconstitutional Legislation* [1913] (New York: Ams Press, 1968).

34. *Munn v. Illinois,* 94 U.S. 113, 134 (1877).

35. This discussion of judicial decision-making axioms is not intended to be comprehensive. A more thorough discussion is available in Abraham, *The Judicial Process,* pp. 354–80.

36. Shapiro, *Freedom of Speech,* p. 28.

37. Quoted in Charles P. Curtis, *Lions Under the Throne* (Boston: Houghton Mifflin, 1947), p. 281.

CHAPTER 6

1. *The Magnificent Yankee* appeared on Broadway in 1951.

2. Roscoe Pound, "Judge Holmes's Contributions to the Science of Law," *Harvard Law Review* 34 (March 1921):449.

3. H. L. Mencken, "Mr. Justice Holmes," in *The Vintage Mencken,* ed. Alistair Cooke (New York: Vintage Books, 1955), p. 190.

4. Ben W. Palmer, "Hobbs, Holmes and Hitler," *American Bar Association Journal* 31 (November 1945):569–73.

5. G. Edward White, "The Rise and Fall of Justice Holmes," *University of Chicago Law Review* 39 (Fall 1971):55.

6. Holmes, "Path of the Law," p. 458.

7. Gilmore, *Ages of American Law,* p. 62.

8. Holmes, "Path of the Law," p. 459.

9. Ibid., p. 458.

10. Ibid., p. 457.

11. Ibid.

12. Ibid.

13. Ibid., p. 458.

14. For a discussion of Holmes's view of the judicial role and its relation to Holmes's belief that law and morals were not the same, *see* Henry M. Hart, Jr., "Holmes' Positivism—An Addendum," *Harvard Law Review* 64 (April 1951):929–39; and Mark DeWolfe Howe, "The Positivism of Mr. Justice Holmes," *Harvard Law Review* 64 (February 1951):529-46.

15. Holmes, "Path of the Law," p. 460.
16. Ibid.
17. Ibid.
18. Ibid., p. 458.
19. Ibid., pp. 464–65.
20. Ibid., p. 465.
21. Ibid.
22. Ibid.
23. Ibid., p. 466.
24. Ibid., p. 459.
25. Ibid., p. 465.
26. Ibid., p. 467.
27. *See* Howard N. Meyer, *The Amendment That Refused to Die* (Boston: Beacon Press, 1978); and Arnold N. Paul, *Conservative Crisis and the Rule of Law: Attitudes of Bar and Bench,* 1887–1895 (New York: Harper Torchbooks, 1969).
28. Richard C. Cortner, *The Supreme Court and the Second Bill of Rights* (Madison: Univ. of Wisconsin Press, 1981), p. 56.
29. Walter Robert Goedecke, *Change and the Law* (Tallahassee: Florida State Univ. Press, 1969), p. 166.
30. Holmes, "Path of the Law," p. 467.
31. Ibid., p. 468.
32. Ibid.
33. Ibid., p. 469.
34. Ibid., p. 470.
35. Ibid., p. 471.

CHAPTER 7

1. *See generally* Holmes, "The Path of the Law."
2. *Marbury v. Madison,* 1 Cr. 137 (1803). See discussion in Chapter 4.
3. It was not until *Gitlow v. New York,* 258 U.S. 652 (1925), that the Court applied the protection of the First Amendment to abridgments emanating from state as well as federal legislation. The doctrine was not used successfully in a freedom of expression case until 1931; *see Stromberg v. California* 283 U.S. 259 (1931); and *Near v. Minnesota* 283 U.S. 697 (1931). The first indication that the Court would consider holding state legislation up to First Amendment standards appeared in a dissenting opinion by Justice John Marshall Harlan in *Patterson v. Colorado,* 205 U.S. 454 (1907).
4. *United States v. Carolene Products,* 304 U.S. 144, 152.
5. *Schenck v. United States,* 249 U.S. 247 (1919).
6. Holmes was an associate justice of the Massachusetts Supreme Court from 1882 to 1899 and served as chief justice from 1899 to 1902.
7. *Hanson v. Globe,* 159 Mass. 293 (1893).
8. Ibid., p. 302.
9. Ibid., p. 100.

10. *Commonwealth v. Davis,* 162 Mass. 510 (1895).
11. Ibid., p. 511.
12. Ibid., p. 512.
13. Ibid.
14. *Northern Securities Co. v. United States,* 193 U.S. 197 (1904).
15. Ibid., pp. 400–401.
16. Ibid., p. 401.
17. Ibid.
18. Ibid., p. 402.
19. *Lochner v. New York,* 198 U.S. 45 (1905).
20. *Allgeyer v. Louisiana,* 165 U.S. 578 (1897).
21. Ibid., p. 589.
22. *Lochner v. New York,* 198 U.S. 45, 75.
23. Ibid., pp. 75–76.
24. Ibid., p. 75.
25. Ibid., p. 76.
26. Ibid.
27. *Patterson v. Colorado,* 205 U.S. 454 (1907).
28. Ibid., p. 460.
29. Ibid., p. 461.
30. Ibid., p. 462.
31. Ibid.
32. *Moyer v. Peabody,* 212 U.S. 78 (1909).
33. Ibid., p. 84. Compare this language with Holmes's statement in *Schenck:* "We admit that in many places and in ordinary times the defendants in saying all that was said . . . would have been within their constitutional rights. But the character of every act depends on the circumstances in which it is done." 249 U.S. 47, 52.
34. Ibid., p. 85.
35. *Baily v. Alabama,* 219 U.S. 219 (1911).
36. Ibid., p. 245.
37. Ibid., p. 246.
38. Ibid., p. 247.
39. Ibid.
40. Ibid., p. 248.
41. *Fox v. Washington,* 236 U.S. 273 (1915).
42. Rem. & Bal. Code, sec. 2564.
43. *Fox v. Washington,* 236 U.S. 273, 276.
44. Ibid., p. 277.
45. Ibid.
46. Ibid., p. 278.
47. *Hammer v. Dagenhart,* 247 U.S. 251 (1917).
48. Ibid. p., 277.
49. Ibid. p., 281.
50. Ibid. p., 280.

CHAPTER 8

1. Cited in Ronald Steel, *Walter Lippmann and the American Century* (Boston: Little. Brown and Co., 1980), p. 124.

2. *See generally* Joseph Robert Conlin, *Bread and Roses Too: Studies of the Wobblies* (Westport, Conn.: Greenwood Pub. Corp., 1969).

3. Nat Henthoff, *The First Freedom: The Tumultuous History of Free Speech in America* (New York: Delacorte Press, 1980), p. 99.

4. *Meyer v. Nebraska*, 262 U.S. 390 (1923).

5. *See generally* John Lofton, *The Press as Guardian of the First Amendment* (Columbia: Univ. of South Carolina Press, 1980); Paul Murphy, *The Meaning of Freedom of Speech: First Amendment Readings from Wilson to FDR* (Westport, Conn.: Greenwood Pub. Co., 1972); William Preston, Jr., *Aliens and Dissenters: Federal Suppression of Radicals 1903-1933* (Cambridge: Harvard Univ. Press, 1963).

6. Holmes, *The Common Law,* p. 5.

7. Holmes, "The Path of the Law," p. 466.

8. Holmes, *The Common Law.*

9. Holmes to Pollock, 23 April 1910, in Mark DeWolf Howe, *Holmes-Pollock Letters,* vol. 1 (Cambridge: Harvard Univ. Press), p. 163.

10. Holmes to Einstein, 31 Oct. 1918, in James Bishop Peabody, ed., *Holmes-Einstein Letters* (New York: St. Martin's Press, 1964), p. 173.

11. Holmes to Einstein, 28 Sept. 1918, Ibid., pp. 171-72.

12. Holmes to Pollock, 23 April 1910, in Howe, *Holmes-Pollock Letters,* vol. 1, p. 163.

13. Barron and Dienes, Handbook of Free Speech, p. 5.

14. H. N. Hirsch, *The Enigma of Felix Frankfurter* (New York: Basic Books, 1981), p. 133.

15. *See generally* Margaret A. Blanchard, "Filling in the Void: Speech and Press in State Courts Prior to *Gitlow,*" *The First Amendment Reconsidered,* ed. Bill Chamberlain and Charlene Brown (New York, 1982), pp. 14-59.

16. Holmes to Laski, 28 Feb. 1919, in Mark DeWolfe Howe, ed., *Holmes-Laski Letters* (Cambridge: Harvard Univ. Press, 1953), p. 186.

17. Holmes to Pollock, 5 April 1919, in Howe, *Holmes-Pollock Letters,* vol. 2 (Cambridge: Harvard Univ. Press, 1961), p. 7.

18. Holmes to Pollock, 27 April 1919, Ibid., p. 11. The "him" in the sentence referred to Debs. Charles Schenck and Elizabeth Baer were those Holmes referred to as "some other poor devils."

19. Holmes to Pollock, 5 April 1919, Ibid., p. 7.

20. Holmes to Laski, 16 March 1919, in Howe, *Holmes-Laski Letters,* p. 190.

21. Holmes to Laski, 16 March 1919. Ibid.

22. Laski to Holmes, 18 March 1919. Ibid., p. 191.

23. Holmes never mailed the letter to Croly, but instead mailed it to Laski with the following explanation: "Yesterday I wrote the within and decided not to send it as some themes may be burning. Instead I entrust it confidentially to you and it will answer your inquiry about Freund. I thought it poor stuff—for reasons within." Holmes to Laski, 13 May 1919. Ibid., p. 202.

24. Ibid., p. 204.
25. Ibid.
26. *Northern Securities Company v. United States,* 193 U.S. 197, 402 (1904).
27. Holmes to Laski, 15 Sept. 1916, in Howe, *Holmes-Laski Letters,* p. 21.

CHAPTER 9

   1. Holmes to Pollock, 1 Jan. 1917, in Howe, *Holmes-Pollock Letters,* vol. 1, p. 245.
   2. *Schenck v. United States,* 249 U.S. 47 (1919).
   3. Ibid., pp. 48–49.
   4. Ibid., p. 49.
   5. Ibid., p. 50.
   6. Ibid., p. 49.
   7. Ibid., p. 50.
   8. Ibid.
   9. Ibid.
  10. Ibid.
  11. Gibbons and Nelson, "Brief of Plaintiffs-in-Error," p. 1018.
  12. *Schenck v. United States,* 249 U.S. 47, 50.
  13. Ibid., p. 49.
  14. Ibid., p. 51.
  15. Ibid.
  16. Ibid.
  17. Gibbons and Nelson, "Brief of Plaintiffs-in-Error," pp. 1018–19.
  18. Holmes, "Path of the Law," p. 462.
  19. Holmes to Laski, 15 Sept. 1916, in Howe, *Holmes-Laski Letters,* p. 21.
  20. Gibbons and Nelson, "Brief of Plaintiffs-in-Error," p. 995.
  21. Ibid.
  22. Ibid.
  23. *Schenck v. United States,* 249 U.S. 47, 52.
  24. Ibid.
  25. *Aikens v. Wisconsin,* 195 U.S. 194 (1904).
  26. Wisconsin Stat. 1898, sec. 4466a.
  27. *See generally* Gilmore, *Ages of American Law.*
  28. *Aikens v. Wisconsin,* 195 U.S. 194, 205–06.
  29. *Schenck v. United States,* 249 U.S. 47, 52.
  30. *Gompers v. Buck Stove and Range Co.,* 221 U.S. 418 (1910).
  31. Ibid., p. 439.
  32. Ibid., p. 437.
  33. *Schenck v. United States,* 249 U.S. 47, 52.
  34. Gibbons and Nelson, "Brief of Plaintiffs-in-Error," p. 996.
  35. Ibid.
  36. Ibid., p. 1002.

37. *Schenck v. United States*, 249 U.S. 47, 51.

38. Ibid., pp. 51–52.

39. Gibbons and Nelson, "Brief of Plaintiffs-in-Error," p. 993.

40. Ibid., p. 994.

41. Holmes to Pollock, 5 April 1919, in Howe, *Holmes-Pollock Letters*, vol. 2, p. 7.

42. *Schenck v. United States*, 249 U.S. 47, 52.

43. Ibid.

44. *Goldman v. United States*, 245 U.S. 474 (1917).

45. Ibid., p. 447.

46. *Schenck v. United States*, 249 U.S. 47, 52.

47. Ibid., p. 52.

48. Ibid.

49. Ibid.

50. Ibid., p. 53.

51. Ibid.

CHAPTER 10

1. "Supreme Court Rules Against Pacifists," *New York Times*, 4 March 1919, p.11; "Sustains 'Spy' Law," *Washington Post*, 4 March 1919, p. 8.

2. Meiklejohn, *Political Freedom*, p. 78.

3. Leo Pfeffe, *This Honorable Court* (Boston: Beacon Press, 1965), p.265.

4. *Schenck v. United States*, 249 U.S. 47, 51.

5. *See* Chapter 7, n. 18, n. 22, and accompanying discussion above.

6. *See* Chapter 6, n. 18, and accompanying discussion above.

7. *See* Chapter 4, n. 27, and accompanying discussion above.

8. "Bomb Injures Ex-Senator's Wife, Maims a Servant," *New York Times*, 30 April 1919, p. 1.

9. "36 Were Marked As Victims By Bomb Conspirers," *New York Times*, 1 May 1919, p. 1.

10. "Find More Bombs Sent In The Mails; One to Overman," *New York Times*, 2 May 1919, p. 1.

11. "Radicals Watched in Bomb Plot Hunt," *New York Times*, 4 May 1919, p. 12.

12. Louis Post, *The Deportation Delirium of 1920* (New York: De Capo Press, 1970), p.46.

13. Ibid, p. 47.

14. *Frohwerk v. United States*, 249 U.S. 204 (1919).

15. Ibid., pp. 208–9.

16. *Debs v. United States*, 249 U.S. 211 (1919).

17. Ibid., p. 214.

18. Ibid., p. 215.

19. *Abrams v. United States*, 250 U.S. 616 (1919); *Schaefer v. United States*, 251 U.S. 466 (1920); *Pierce v. United States*, 252 U.S. 239 (1920).

20. *See generally* Yosal Rogat and James O'Fallon, "Mr. Justice Holmes: A Dis-

senting Opinion—The Speech Cases," *Stanford Law Review*, 36 (July 1984):1349–1406.

21. *Abrams v. United States*, 250 U.S. 616, 618–9.

22. Ibid., p. 228.

23. Ibid.

24. Ibid., p. 616.

25. Ibid., pp. 630–31.

26. *De Jong v. Oregon*, 299 U.S. 353, 364–5 (1937).

27. Testimony given before the Rules Committee of the House of Representatives, 29 January 1920. In *Do We Need More Sedition Laws?* (New York: American Civil Liberties Union), p. 6.

28. Ibid., p. 4.

29. O'Brian, "New Encroachments on Individual Freedom," p. 3.

30. Ibid., p. 2.

31. Gilman G. Udell, comp., *Laws Relating to Espionage, Sabotage, Etc.* (Washington, D.C.: U.S. Government Printing Office, 1976).

32. *Meese v. Keene*, No. 85–1180, 28 April 1987.

33. File No. A11 644 708, In the Matter of Margaret Jo Randall, respondent in deportation proceedings; 28 August 1986, U.S. Department of Justice, Executive Office for Immigration Review, Office of Immigration Judge, El Paso, Texas, p. 24. *See also* "Writers Protest U.S. Order to Deport Author Over Political Works," *New York Times*, 16 Nov. 1986, p.15.

34. Anthony Lewis, "U.S. Treatment of Journalists an Embarrassment to Americans," *Los Angeles Daily Journal*, 3 Dec. 1986, p. 4.

35. *See generally* Bob Woodward, *Veil: The Secret Wars of the CIA, 1981–1987* (New York: Simon and Schuster, 1987).

36. Speech before the Practicing Law Institute's Communications Law Seminar, 14 Nov. 1986, New York City.

Index